# How to
# Think about the
# Economy

## A PRIMER

### PER L. BYLUND

MISESINSTITUTE
AUBURN, ALABAMA

How to
Think about the
# Economy

Mr. Steven G. Farrall, Mr. Peter Francis Fenwick, Col. James Finger

Willard and Donna Fischer, Mr. David Fligel

Mr. Bo Fredricsson, in Memory of Murray Rothbard

Mr. and Mrs. David Fusato, Mr. Steve Gamble, Mr. Christopher Georgacas

Dr. Elizabeth Gesenhues, Mr. Gary Halpin, Mr. Charles F. Hanes

Mr. and Mrs. Jeffrey Harding, Mr. Charles Howard Hartman

Mr. Jeff Hattem, in Honor of Per Bylund, Mr. Sheldon Hayer

Mr. William N. Haynes, Mr. Michael Heil, Sassan S. Hejazi, PhD

Dr. Frederic H. Herman, Mr. Nathan Hines

Mr. and Mrs. Allen D. Houtz, in Honor of Micah L. Houtz

Dr. Stefan Hubrich, Mr. Jeffrey J. Jean

Mr. Quest Jelinek, in Honor of Chris Jelinek

Mr. Dan Johnson and Ms. Randee Laskewitz, Mr. Wesley Johnson

Mr. Franklin Keller, Dr. Matthias G. Kelm

Mr. Tam Kemabonta, in Honor of Abiye Geoffrey

Mr. and Mrs. James E. Klingler, Mr. Alexandros Konstantinidis

Mr. Lawrence Lahusen, Mr. Stephan Livera, Mr. Donald Lovelace

Douglas J. Mackenzie, MD, in Memory of Joseph R. Mackenzie

Mr. Bruce S. Markel III

Dr. and Mrs. Charles W. Martin, in Honor of our grandsons:

Tom III, Will, and Henry Strandwitz

Mr. Ralph Martins, Mr. and Mrs. Joseph Matarese, Mr. Chester McKinney, Jr.

Mr. Lonnie McQuirter, Mr. Kevin Menard, Mr. Mauro Miranda, CFA, FRM

Mr. Brian Moore, Dr. Lyle E. Muller, Mr. Gary J. Myre, Mr. Ernest L. Ortiz

Mr. Andrew Packer, Mr. Michael Page, Mr. Scott M. Parks, Mr. Brian Paulsen

Mr. Steven Potter, Mr. Joel Price, Mr. T. James Reynolds

Mr. Scott Richardson, Ms. Joan Riemer, Mr. Jorge F. Roca Arteta

Mr. Patrick Rosenwald, in Honor of Sofia Rosenwald

Mr. Thomas S. Ross, Mr. Gabe L. Royer

Mr. Timothy Rozmajzl, in Memory of R. Nelson Nash

Dr. Murray Sabrin, Mr. Keith Sarbaugh, David and Elaine Sarosi

Mr. William P. Sarubbi, Mr. William Schnuckel, Mr. Kenneth L. Schweitzer

Mr. Stephen C. Sebastian, Dr. Prakash Seshadri

Mr. Jack Seward, Jr., Mr. Brian Sharpe

Dr. and Mrs. Paul L. Shetler, in Memory of Captain Martin Greene, US Army

Mrs. Lorraine Smith, in Memory of Geoffrey Stansfield

Dr. and Mrs. G. Keith Smith, Mr. Jay L. Smith, Mr. Craig Stasi

Mr. Richard L. Stees, Mr. Edward Stikeleather, Mr. Byron L. Stoeser

Mr. Emanuel Mark Strategos, Mr. Timothy Streid

Drs. Benjamin and Rosanne Thurman, Mr. Gregory James Tisdale

Mr. Peter Towers, Mr. Thomas E. Verkuilen, Dr. James H. Vernier

Mr. Reginald Victoria, Mr. Joe Vierra, The Villers Family

Mr. Mark Walker, Mr. C. David Walker

Mr. Skippy Weil, in Memory of Martin Luther King

Mr. Donald G. Weiss, in Memory of Richard Ogden Weiss

Mr. Matt Wesley, Mr. Bryant Williams, Mr. Jerry K. Williams

Richard and Susan Williams, Kirby and Andra Wisian

Malcolm and Gerlinde Wittig, Mr. William B. Zieburtz, Jr.

*To Carl Menger, Ludwig von Mises, and the other giants upon whose shoulders I have the great honor of standing.*

THE MISES INSTITUTE, founded in 1982, is an education and research center for the study of Austrian economics. In support of the school of thought represented by Ludwig von Mises, Murray N. Rothbard, Henry Hazlitt, and F.A. Hayek, we publish books and journals, sponsor student and professional conferences, and provide online education. Mises.org is a vast resource of free material for anyone in the world interested in these ideas. We advocate a radical shift in the intellectual climate, away from statism and toward a private property order.

For more information, see mises.org, write us at info@mises.org, or phone us at 1.800.OF.MISES.

*Published 2022 by the Mises Institute*

518 West Magnolia Avenue
Auburn, Alabama 36832
mises.org

ISBN: 978-1-61016-755-0

# Contents

# Preface

This little book was written to accomplish something big: economic literacy. It is intentionally kept very short to be inviting rather than intimidating, as economics books typically are. If I managed to meet this bar, you, the reader, will gain life-changing understanding of how the economy works in practically no time. This is lots of value at a very low cost.

If I have managed to exceed expectations, this book will also make you *excited* about what economics has to offer. Because economic literacy is mind-opening. Sound economic reasoning is an enormously powerful tool for understanding both the economy and society. It uncovers what is going on under the surface and why things are the way they are. In fact, economic literacy is *necessary* to properly understand the world.

But it is also quite possible that I have failed in my undertaking. If so, I would appreciate if you would tell me what you think I have done wrong and how I could have done it better. I'm easy to find online, so please share your comments with me. Please pass the book on to someone else. They might have better luck and get more out of it. At any rate, the book should not have set you back much—it's pretty cheap. And maybe you still learned something?

In preparing this manuscript, I have benefited from discussions, feedback, and suggestions from many people. Special thanks go to Porter Burkett, Susanne Bylund, Richard Gajan, David Gordon, Jonathan Newman, and Mikael Nordin, who provided feedback on previous drafts of the manuscript. Any errors that still remain are entirely my own fault.

My sincere thanks also to the many people who generously donated to make this book possible and to the Mises Institute for giving me this opportunity to make Austrian economic theory available to the general public in a short, accessible, and easy-to-understand format.

Per Bylund
Tulsa, Oklahoma
July 2022

# PART I

# Economics

# CHAPTER 1

# What Economics Is

Economics is an exciting field.

The economics of old sought to uncover how the world works. It showed, or even proved, that there is a natural order to it. There is structure to the apparent chaos. The economy has something of a life of its own: it has a nature. This means not only that we can study it and learn about its ways, but also that we are not free to tamper with it at will and cannot make it work in ways that we might prefer but that are not in line with its nature. There are "laws" by which the economy works, and they are immutable. Economics over the past three centuries has been about identifying, learning, and understanding those laws.

Core to understanding the economy is recognizing that it is about human actions and interactions. In fact, the economy *is* people acting and interacting. It is little or nothing else. We tend to think of the economy in terms of resources, machines, businesses, and perhaps jobs. But that is a simplification that is misleading. Those are important, but they are all means to ends. The economy is about *using means to attain ends*. To put it differently, it is how we act to satisfy our wants, to make us better off. Simply put, the economy is about creating value.

Our means are limited but our wants are not. We must figure out how to make as much as possible with the little we have. If we choose to pursue one end, then we cannot use the same means to pursue other ends as well. In other words, there is always a tradeoff. Every choice we make and every action we take means that we forego what we did not choose. Either you take the car for a drive or you stay at home. You cannot do both at the same time. You can use your money to buy one thing, or to buy another. Or you can save your money for another time. But the same money cannot be used both to buy something and be saved too. Your choice of one thing means you did not and cannot choose the other. By choosing one thing over another, by *acting*, we rank things' value to us—we *economize*. The economy is all of us economizing.

## The Economy

The economy is an unplanned order. It is what emerges when people go about their own business, when we act and interact as we see fit.

The French nineteenth-century economist Frédéric Bastiat captured this in a question: "How does Paris get fed?" Living in a large city, Parisians do not produce food but still have abundant access to it. The important question is how this comes to be. After all, there is no central plan for what types and quantities of foods are to be offered to Parisians and when. There is no one telling farmers when and what to sow, which land to use for each crop, what tools to use or develop, or in

what cities, towns, or market squares to sell their produce and at what prices. All of this *just happens*. The
economy is a decentralized and distributed system
where all people—farmers and city folk alike—make
their own plans and decisions. They do not simply
carry out orders from some central command.[1]

The aim of economics is to understand how an
economy, in all its shapes and forms, works: the nature
and workings of the overall process of people making
their own decisions, acting, and interacting as they see
fit. The economy lacks both plan and planner. It doesn't
even have a goal. It just is.

But people have goals. They have needs and wants
that they strive to satisfy using different means. Some
things are provided by nature, but most of them require
that people exert effort to produce them. These are the
goods and services that satisfy whatever wants we have.
Production is core to the economy: it is about providing as many means as possible to satisfy as many highly
valued wants as possible

## The Economic Problem

Production is a problem. It is not simply a matter of
how many resources are available. There is no constant
relationship between input and output. Very often
more inputs can produce more outputs, it is true. But

---

[1]In many economies, the government plays a large role, which is often
in the form of a central command. We will discuss this issue in Sec-
tion 3. For now, we will be focusing on the economy itself—i.e., how
things come to work out on their own and without central command
or plan.

with innovations we get more output per input—we increase productivity. This is even more obvious when we talk about the *value* of the output and not just the quantity. Value is never automatic. One can use a lot of resources to produce something that turns out to be pretty worthless. If I produce a painting, the expected result would be of little value regardless of my effort or how much paint I use. The same canvas and paint used by Vincent van Gogh would create something of much higher value. By placing his signature on my painting it would increase my painting's value. But my signature on his painting would decrease its value.

The only relationship that exists between inputs and outputs is that inputs must be used to produce outputs. We cannot create something out of nothing.

The economic problem is not production *per se* but economizing production. It is about the issue that arises because we do not have more resources than we can find uses for. In other words, resources are scarce. So it is incumbent upon us to figure out how our resources can be used to produce the best possible outcome (in value terms). We have become increasingly good at figuring this out, especially in the last few centuries. For thousands of years, we made very little progress, but suddenly, with what is referred to as industrialization, nation after nation began lifting itself out of poverty through breakthroughs in production. The interest in economics coincides with this development.

Hence the title of Adam Smith's hugely influential treatise: *An Inquiry into the Nature and Causes of the Wealth of Nations*. The title brings attention to the two dimensions of national wealth (prosperity) that are still core to economics: the *nature* of wealth and its *causes*. The nature of wealth refers to how we should understand it, what comprises it, and how the economy as a system relates to the theory of value as personal satisfaction. The causes of wealth refers to the origins and the particular processes that brought this prosperity about. If we understand them properly, we can lift people out of poverty and create an ever more prosperous society.

Economics as the study of how the economy works is consequently also the science of how prosperity is created.

## Economics as Understanding

To be an economist is to be a student of the economy as an ongoing process. The aim is to understand how it works and its nature. It is about figuring out the nature and causes of those universal processes, mechanisms, and orders that we identify as the economy. From this we learn about prosperity and, importantly, how to produce more of it and make sure more people benefit from it.

To form an understanding of how the economy works, we must be humble before the fact that it exists and there is an order to it—it has a *nature*. The task of the economist is not to predict the specifics of the future but to uncover the underlying processes that produce the economic outcomes that we can observe. In other words, we must develop a logic for understanding aggregate economic phenomena and behavior—an economic *theory*. Economics is a framework for *how to think and reason about the economy*, for making sense of what is going on. An "intuition," if you will.

It follows that learning economics is fundamentally about gaining economic literacy so we can better understand the world we are part of. The *real* world, not the invented world we find in formalized models. As Ludwig von Mises put it, "Economics deals with real man, weak and subject to error as he is, not with ideal beings, omniscient and perfect as only gods could be." Yes, exactly.

# Chapter 2

# Economic Theory

Like other sciences and fields of study, economics is a body of theory. Theory is a collection of explanations that allows us to understand something. Economic theory allows us to *understand how an economy works*. It explains the workings of the economy as a whole so that we can understand the meaning, impact, origins, and evolution of economic phenomena.

For theory to be reliable and useful, it must provide a coherent picture. If it doesn't, then some of its explanations are contradictory. Contradictions are a sign that something is wrong. So, the body of a theory must be logically stringent and must make up a consistent whole. This means it must be consistent with the basic assumptions on which it rests—it must be true to first principles.

But it is not enough to produce a consistent whole based on first principles if those principles are themselves flawed. After all, it is possible to produce an internally consistent theory based on faulty assumptions. Such systems can appear very convincing because they are consistent, but they still fail to provide real understanding because every explanation hinges on something that is not true and is perhaps not even reasonable. You would not want to cross a bridge designed by an engineer who believes paper is stronger than iron. It doesn't matter how accurate the math used is or how sophisticated the design—the assumption is wrong and therefore the bridge is not reliable. It cannot hold the expected weight even if all the calculations are accurate. The same is true with economic theory: it must be built on solid principles and reliable assumptions.

Consequently, for a theory to properly explain how the world works, it must be internally consistent *and* based on true assumptions. A theory cannot meet only one of those criteria and still provide us with real understanding of the world; it must meet both.

## The Starting Point

Economics is based in the concept of human action as purposeful behavior. What this means is that when people act, they try to achieve something. It does not mean that they are always accurate or do the "right thing" (whatever that is). But it means the reason they try to achieve it is that they *value* the expected outcome in some way. What they value, why they value it, and whether it is reasonable or rational to do so is irrelevant. Such things lie beyond the scope of economic theory. What matters is that their action is motivated by the expected outcome.

It may appear strange that economics does not deal with why people value some things but not others. But it does not. People's dreams, fantasies, and imaginations only have economic relevance if they are *acted upon*. After all, if you have a dream that you do not act on, you are not making it happen. It remains but a dream. The dream itself makes no difference in the world; merely wishing does not make it real.

So, action is a rather logical starting point for studying social reality. Acting is how we make changes to the world.

## Unpacking Human Action

Recognizing action for what it is—purposeful behavior—is surprisingly powerful. It provides us with insights about human affairs far beyond what most people think possible. In fact, the economist Ludwig von Mises showed that economic theory can be derived from this simple concept.

Lets look at the types of things we can learn about the world simply from elaborating on what human action means. We have already pointed out that actions are taken for some purpose that makes sense to the actor. We know that actions are directed toward attaining something—some outcome—that the actor considers beneficial. In other words, actions are intended to achieve something the actor personally values.

Because actors are trying to achieve something, it follows that they have not already attained it and take actions in order to become better off than they already are. Consequently, we conclude that there are things actors want that they do not have but they think they can attain by taking an action that they believe would make them better off. In other words, actions are fundamentally *causal*: we act because we believe that we can bring about a specific change.

We also conclude that actors think their action is the best or only way to attain the outcome. Why else would they undertake the action? That they have not already done so suggests that they either were unaware of the possibility, lacked the means to act on it, or ranked other ends higher. All of these suggest scarcity—that there are insufficient means to satisfy all the wants held—and that the actor makes choices. That the actor must choose implies that he or she must make tradeoffs. In other words, the actor *economizes*.

We can also conclude that human action is in fact always *individual* action motivated by some personally valued end and taken toward that end. Other individuals may have the same outcome in mind, and to be feasible an action might require collaboration, but this does not change the fact that each person acts. People may choose to act in concert, but those are individual choices. The group itself does not act. That four people collaborate to lift and move a piano does not mean that the group lifted the piano but that the four people coordinated their individual efforts toward that common end. In other words, economics is *methodologically individualist*.

Things like business firms, groups, and governments exist and have a real effect on how people act. But we cannot understand how without also recognizing that the people *in* firms, groups, and governments act. By recognizing this, we understand that actors within groups may have goals that contradict the group's stated goals and therefore there are tensions and some people may act in ways that undermine the group's stated goals. This would not be possible had we assumed that the group itself acts.

## THE GENIUS OF THE ACTION AXIOM

Economics uses logical reasoning to uncover the processes that make up the economy and it recognizes that the motivation for action is personal—that *value is subjective*. Value subjectivity allows economists to formulate a realistic and reliable theory that explains prices as a result of personal valuations on the margin. Because individuals choose between actions, they must rank their options. They do so subjectively, based on the anticipated value that they expect the action's outcome will provide them.

We never value things in themselves, but for the satisfaction we think they can provide us. A glass of water in the desert is probably more satisfying than a glass of water while loafing on the couch at home. Why? Because we value things by the satisfaction they can give us in the situation we are in. When loafing on the couch, the greatest satisfaction we can get from a glass of water is not nearly as high as when trying to stay hydrated and alive in a desert. And the more we have of something, the lesser the satisfaction of using another one. In fact, each unit of something is valued at the satisfaction we can get out of the last (marginal) unit. So in any situation, if we have three glasses of water, we value each of them less than if we had only two. But more than if we had had four. Because the value to us of any one glass is the satisfaction it contributes—the lowest and marginal value. That's why we act differently depending on how many we have of something and how important those things are to us—what satisfactions we expect to get from them.

In other words, action connects the subjective valuations that are in our heads—our rankings of the possible outcomes of our actions—with the things that exist outside our minds. Action is the bridge between personal valuations, which cannot be measured and outcomes in the real world. By understanding action as the starting point of economic reasoning, the fact that value is subjective poses no problem for understanding the production of goods and services and other economic phenomena. We do not have to know what or why people value, only that they do. And that they act accordingly.

All economic phenomena—resource allocations, market prices, business cycles—are outcomes of human actions, which we know are always purposeful and economizing. The task for economics is therefore to understand the economy and everything it entails from the perspective of the ultimate cause: action.

CHAPTER 3

# How to Do Economics

Economics is often faulted for being "ideological"—for *promoting free markets*. This is a misunderstanding.

The free market in economics is a model—an analytical tool. It excludes complicating circumstances and influences and allows us to study core economic phenomena *on their own* so that they are not mistaken for other effects. In economics, we are interested in understanding the nature and relationships of economic forces. In other words, we exclude things that hamper the economy, such as regulations, that impose upon people's behavior and therefore economic outcomes. The result is an economy where only economic forces are at play—a "free market."

The free-market model serves the same purpose as studying objects in free fall in physics. The free-fall model excludes such things as air resistance in order to study the effects of gravitational pull. It would not be possible to study gravitational pull without separating it from other forces that also have an effect on objects, and may add to or subtract from the effect of gravity. Economics uses the model of the unhampered or free market in the same way: to study economic forces without the influence of other things. We must know how the economy itself works before we can study influences on it.

Economics promotes and advocates free markets as much as physics promotes free-fall. Economic reasoning cannot do without the free-market model.

## THE MEANING OF EXCHANGE

Economics relies on economic reasoning—the use of logic to figure out the why/why-not and when/when-not. It is how we make sense of what we see and uncover the underlying economic processes. Let's illustrate with the example of a basic exchange transaction between two individuals, Adam and Beth.

Let's say Adam offers Beth an apple and Beth gives Adam a quart of milk in return. There are two ways we can analyze this exchange. One is to study it empirically by observing the exchange in real life and collecting "objective," that is, measurable data before, during, and after the exchange. Using these data, we can then describe what took place and look for an explanation.

There is no need to get into specifics to see how this method is unsuitable to understand the meaning of exchange for economic reasoning. Even studying the empirical exchange in detail, we could not uncover *why* the apple shifted from Adam's into Beth's possession, why the milk moved the other way, or even if those two transfers are related to each other. There is no meaning to the observable data; they cannot tell us anything in addition to the bare observable facts of who possesses what and when. Strictly speaking, the data cannot even tell us there was an *exchange*.

Economics is about more than offering descriptions such as "Adam has an apple and Beth has milk" and that a minute later "Beth has the apple and Adam has the milk." It is about understanding that this was an exchange and what exchanging means to the participating parties. We know it must mean something because they *chose* to do it. The exchange was not simply the outcome of certain external stimuli. Exchange is not automatic.

But to study this, we must reason from our understanding of what Adam and Beth are doing. In other words, we recognize—using what we call a priori understanding—that both of them are in fact *acting* and therefore that they are trying to accomplish something. Human action, as Ludwig von Mises reminds us, is purposeful behavior.

With this understanding, we can easily see that this is in fact an exchange: Adam traded his apple for Beth's milk. Because Adam and Beth exchanged goods, we also know that—unless one of them was coerced or defrauded—they both expected to be better off with what they received in exchange. So, they exchanged *because* Adam values the milk higher than the apple *and* Beth values the apple higher than the milk.

This conclusion might appear obvious, and it should: we all have this basic understanding of human action as a purposeful undertaking to attain some end that we expect to be of greater value. We act because we want some change and because we think that change will be better in some sense.

Based on this basic understanding, we make sense of Adam and Beth's exchange. We might not agree with their valuations, but we do not need to. We still understand that voluntary exchange must be based on the parties' "double coincidence of wants"—that both Adam and Beth expected to become better off from the exchange (or they would not have chosen to do it).

## PRICE AND VALUE

In our example, Adam and Beth were unhampered in their economic exchange—a free-market transaction. It's a highly simplified example, but simplifying is not a problem. It is an advantage because it allows us to identify the core processes and mechanisms. We would not have gained any additional understanding by complicating the exchange example with regulations, license requirements, legal definitions, health directives, taxes, etc. Including those things would in fact have made it more difficult to figure out what was actually going on. There would have been too many things involved that could have affected Adam and Beth's decision-making.

So it makes sense to study the exchange, as just an exchange without complicating factors, so that we can learn the meaning of the exchange as such. This also means we can add more factors to see how they change the outcome and learn how those factors relate to, or impact, the exchange. We do this step by step, starting from the core and then adding additional factors. If we do not understand the exchange itself, then we cannot understand how other things affect it either.

Perhaps Beth is a dairy farmer who really likes the apples that Adam grows in his orchard and would be willing to exchange up to a whole gallon (four quarts) of milk to get a single apple. Maybe she thinks Adam's apples are that good. "Paying" a quart is therefore a great deal for her. No wonder she is okay with the exchange!

But the same is also true the other way around. We must conclude that Adam too considers one quart a good "price" to then go through with the exchange. He values one quart of Beth's milk higher than the one apple. If he didn't, the exchange would not take place. So while it is true that Adam could have received more milk for the apple—four times as much—the quart he gets obviously makes the exchange worth his while. Perhaps he would have been willing to pay two apples for a quart of milk. Then paying only one apple is still a good deal from the perspective of his personal valuation.

But we do not need to know Adam and Beth's actual valuations. In fact, they will not need to know this themselves. All that matters is that they both consider the exchange "worth it." The "price" they pay will not be higher than their valuation of what they get in return. For instance, if Adam would not have accepted anything under five quarts of milk for an apple, then there would have been no exchange. Because that wouldn't be worth it to Beth.

Seems obvious? Yes, but we have learned a lot by elaborating on what must be the case for an exchange to happen. We have established the necessary conditions for exchange (both parties must expect to gain from it, the "price" they each pay cannot be higher than their respective valuations of what they get in return) and distinguished between voluntary exchange, which must be for mutual gain, and involuntary transfer (such as theft). While we haven't elaborated on the latter, it's easy to see that neither party, or both, would go through with an exchange that is not to their benefit unless coerced. Or if they are tricked somehow or there is fraud involved.

## Price Mechanism

Let's add a third person, Charlie, who grows pears. Beth fancies this delicious novelty and gladly trades all her milk for a full basket of pears. That's three gallons (twelve quarts) for fifteen pears. Adam then comes along and tries to repeat yesterday's exchange with Beth, but Beth is already out of milk. The following day, Adam visits Beth earlier to get a chance to "buy" milk before Charlie gets it all. Beth likes Charlie's pears better than apples, but Adam says he's willing to offer Beth *two* apples for a quart of milk. Since her milk now buys twice as many apples as before, she considers it.

This simple example is now providing insight into how the *price mechanism* works. Prices are exchange ratios. They are not determined at random but by people's ranking of different goods. We can see that there are limits to where the prices might end up. Beth's limit is a gallon of milk per apple. She doesn't think paying more would be worth it. But with the new opportunity to exchange for pears, Beth no longer considers apples worth buying even at the price of one quart of milk. This is obvious from her buying only pears yesterday. Her valuation of an apple might not have changed, but she values the deal she can get for pears higher. Our purchasing decisions are based on such comparisons of value. They are relative: we pursue what we value most, and the prices we pay are limited by our valuation of what we get and what we offer as payment.

We can use this example to establish what the free-market exchange ratios (prices) between apples, pears, and milk would be, given Adam, Beth, and Charlie's current valuations. To Beth, it is worth it to exchange one quart of milk for one apple. But not if she can get five pears for a gallon of milk—that is a better deal for her. Adam is now offering two apples for each quart of milk, which Beth is considering. If she takes the deal, then it would appear Beth values pears somewhere between one and two apples. We cannot be more exact than this, even if we assume that Beth's taste for apples and pears doesn't change. What we can do is record the exchange ratios over time. It seems an apple exchanged at one quart of milk on day one, five pears exchanged for a gallon of milk on day two, and two apples exchanged for a quart of milk on day three. But we did not observe and do not know anything about the limits of the three people's valuations. Or how they could have changed over time.

This is the logic of prices. Add more people and more goods, and it will be more difficult to keep track of everybody and everything. But the mechanism is the same. Prices are exchange ratios. This is true even if everybody starts using one of the goods as a common medium of exchange, for example, money. If everybody starts referring to prices of goods in terms of how much milk it takes to buy them, then it will be much easier to compare prices. But prices are still exchange ratios and exchanges are still for mutual gain.

## THE STEP-BY-STEP METHOD

Practically all of the important information that we get from the example of Adam, Beth, and Charlie was based not on observation but on our prior understanding of human action. Because we understand that we act to attain something that we value and that we engage in exchange with others for mutual gain, we can uncover the meaning of Adam's, Beth's, and Charlie's exchanges and the exchange ratios that they determine. Simply observing who has what when, and perhaps the "mechanics" of the exchange, is not enough to understand what is going on. Similarly, in the economy overall: we cannot make two observations and pretend to have learned the processes that caused a difference between them. We have to step through the logic of action to uncover what actually was going on.

Let's jump ahead and consider an example of a money economy (we'll discuss money in chapter 6). Money has a certain purchasing power: we need specific amounts to buy different types of goods. Many economists, both past and present, would correctly claim that the supply of money (how much money is available) affects the prices of goods. As new money is created there is more money to buy the same number of goods, so money prices tend to go up. If the number of goods available to buy is the same but the money supply instead falls, then money is harder to come by—so money prices tend to fall.

But this does not mean we can also conclude that there is a proportional relationship between money supply and goods prices. Doubling the supply of money will not double all prices. In fact, even if we magically doubled all money overnight so that when people wake up the next day they find the amount of money in every bank account, wallet, and mattress has doubled, we still could not say the prices of all goods would double. Why not? Because people do not react in the same way or at the same time to the doubling of their cash. The new prices, just like the old, will be determined by people's actions.

To use proper economic reasoning we must walk through the logic *step by step* to fully take into account the changes that happen over time and in sequence. We know that prices are exchange ratios, determined by supply (how much is offered for sale) and demand (how much people are willing to buy). But doubling a person's cash on hand does not mean they will double their purchases of the same goods. Instead, they will always act to purchase the goods that best satisfy their wants relative to the other goods available.

To put it differently, if people had purchased two pounds of butter before their cash doubled, there is no reason for us to expect them to purchase *four* pounds of butter. It is more likely that there are other goods that would satisfy their wants more than a third and a fourth pound of butter and they would then act to purchase those instead. After all, there is a reason they didn't buy the third pound of butter before. In any situation, as we have learned, individuals will pursue whatever ends they consider of greatest value to them.

Just like Beth in the example above chose pears over apples and then apples over pears when Adam offered her a better deal. People waking up with more cash are going to pursue whatever purchases they think will make them best off. Some may choose to simply buy more of the same; others may choose to buy other things in addition to what they usually buy; yet others will buy different things entirely. This means demand for the specific goods offered for sale will change in different ways: some goods will see increased demand, some will see a decrease, and others might see no or little change. This changes their market prices. Increased demand will make the prices of some goods rise and vice versa.

Individuals do not always act at the same time: some will act sooner and before prices have adjusted, which means their purchasing power, given the prices of goods, has in fact doubled. Their actual purchases (their demand) will influence the prices of the goods they buy, which means those acting later may be faced with higher prices *for those goods the earlier actors chose to buy*. Prices are determined by people's actions, not by a mathematical formula.

Imagine if the people above acted early but did not buy another two pounds of butter with their extra money. Instead, they spend it on candy. This means this candy is already sold when those acting later want to buy it. Whatever candy is left for sale is scarcer and the prudent store owner might raise the price to take advantage of this sudden increase in demand. As a result, the later actors will face different price situations than the earlier actors, with some prices being higher and other prices not—some perhaps being lower than they otherwise would have been. Their actions will depend on the specific exchanges they face, but there is no reason to assume that people's actions overall will mysteriously balance out such that all prices end up exactly double what they were the day before. What we can conclude is that prices overall will tend to go up because there is more money but not more goods. But prices of all goods will not rise proportionally with the supply of money.

This step-by-step analysis reveals that the common conclusion that doubling the amount of money will double all prices is premature and unfounded. Prices adjust unevenly and at different times. Consequently, it would be an error to say that money is "neutral" in the economy. Even magical money is not neutral.

## ECONOMICS AS A SOCIAL SCIENCE

The step-by-step analysis of economic reasoning highlights a major difference between social sciences like economics and the natural sciences like chemistry or geology. We simply cannot rely on observation and measurement to gain understanding of social phenomena, and we also cannot rely on static analysis or aggregates. It is necessary to view the economy *as a process*—an evolving complex adaptive system—and walk through the logic step by step to uncover the processes and the real effects as they play out over time.

This means theory in the social sciences has a specific role and meaning that differs from its use in the natural sciences. Theory is *prior* to observation and allows us to make sense of what we are seeing, not the other way around. Theory provides us with a framework to *understand* what we are seeing by uncovering the underlying processes, but it cannot be used to predict precise outcomes. To make predictions as in the natural sciences, we would need to know people's actual subjective valuations, see what they see and how they understand their situation. But none of this is available to us as observers.

Consequently, social science, and therefore economics, is necessarily theoretical in a different sense than the natural sciences. Theory comprises what can be logically derived from human action—it is our explanation of all social phenomena based on our understanding of what it means to act. After all, all social phenomena have this in common: they are the result of people's actions.

This means that theory in the social sciences is more limited in scope than theory in the natural sciences, but it also meets a much higher bar: social science theory is *true*, not merely hypotheses yet to be falsified.

PART II

# Market

CHAPTER 4

# A Process,
# Not a Factory

To help us understand what is going on in the economy, what is important is not the types and number of goods that sit on store shelves. It is why and how they got there.

To answer this question is not simply a matter of pointing out that they arrived by truck last week, because that only tells us about how they were transported to the store. This doesn't tell us anything about all the steps that had to happen to make them available. And there is a lot that takes place before a good is available to buy in a store. Every good you see on a store shelf was originally thought of by someone; it was designed and then produced. The production process was developed, all its operations and the necessary machines and tools engineered, and then the process was overseen and managed. Someone had to think about how best to market and sell the goods to the store and solve the problems of logistics. And someone had to finance the whole thing.

In other words, to understand everything we see around us, including everything that we take for granted, we must recognize that the economy is not a state but a *process*. Looking at a snapshot of the economy tells us very little—if anything—about how it works but can instead mislead us and allow us to jump to conclusions. Without recognizing the process, it can be easy to conclude that a specific situation is inefficient, wrong, or unfair and also to think that it is easy to improve upon it, right the wrong, or calculate an outcome that is less unfair.

For example, if we only look at a portion of the picture, it can seem unfair that the storekeeper has so many goods and other people have none. But looking at the full picture, we realize that these goods are not the storekeeper's to use but are merely goods in progress to their final use with consumers. The storekeeper is not a hoarder—and has little "economic power." The storekeeper is providing the service of making those goods available to consumers and depends on their willingness and ability to buy the goods to make ends meet. Without the store, the customers would need to buy each and every item in bulk from a wholesaler. The storekeeper offer us convenience of many goods in one place.

## A Coordinated Process

There is more to the economy than the production of a good that we see sitting on a store shelf. Its production was possible because there exist other processes and production. For example, a producer of candy usually does not produce the sugar, flavoring, or coloring that is in it. Candy producers rarely produce the machines they use to make the candy; the building where they produce, package, and prepare the candy for shipping; the powerplant to supply them with electricity. It is not enough to say that candy is produced by only one person before it ends up on the store shelves. In fact, candy producers could not make their candy if there were not already producers of the necessary ingredients already available.

In sum, the candy producer is part of a much longer supply chain that fills the gaps in the overall production process, itself comprising lots of producers and specific production processes. Together, these processes—often carried out by different businesses—make a very long chain of operations that step by step produces the specific good from the "original factors" that were available to us at the dawn of time: nature and labor power. Someone cleared the land to grow sugar cane or corn. Someone decided to provide transportation services, which was possible because someone else had already paved roads and manufactured trucks. Those trucks could be manufactured because someone was already producing steel, plastics, and everything else trucks are made of. The steel could be produced because others were running mines and smelting plants. If we were to list all the things that allow the candy maker to make candy, it would be a long list. Even small things like the coffee that the candy factory workers drink on their break is the result of a long supply chain involving thousands of people in many countries. What is important is not to map out all the things that are involved in making a certain good, but to understand that the economy is all of these things *working together*.

It would appear it takes many businesses and workers to produce the long line of goods intended only to make that candy, that you can then purchase. That is true in some sense—they were all involved and all of them were necessary for the final good to be made available to you. But the miner of course has no idea that the ore taken out of the mine will become the steel that is smelted into a part of a machine that produces the candy you can buy in the store today. The coffee bean grower had no idea that his coffee would fuel workers in a faraway country making a special type of candy that your're considering buying. In the same way, the storekeeper doesn't need to know anything about all of the steps that have taken place before there can be a supply of candy to stock on the store shelves.

The point is that the elaborate, complex production process that produces any good you see in the store is not the design of anyone in particular. The overall process is not coordinated around producing specific goods. No one made a blueprint or flow chart specifying all of these steps and their order. No one estimated how much rock needs to be crushed to produce the iron ore that eventually is used in the production of candy. What drives the process is not the creation of goods, but the creation of value for you as a consumer.

Throughout the economy, businesses compete with each other to produce as much value as possible by producing and offering goods. We think of this as competition, the producing of the same or similar items: competing candy makers, for example. But that is a very narrow view. Candy makers indirectly compete for the steel that is used in their candy machines, which means they compete with all other producers that use steel. The same with sugar. And workers. And the coffee that the workers drink, maybe some of them even use sugar in their coffee.

Why does some of the steel produced go to the machines that produce candy? The answer to this question will be discussed at length in chapter 5. Right now, it is sufficient to note that all businesses are involved in producing, directly or indirectly, goods that are intended for consumers. All of production has this aim, whether or not producers of steel, for example, know exactly what their steel is going to be used for. They do not know and don't need to. It is the value that consumers see in those goods produced that determines how much they will be willing to pay. That payment is what justifies the businesses' investments and expenses throughout the economy. Consequently, what indirectly coordinates what all businesses do—and how they do it—is their expectation that they are contributing to providing consumers with valued goods.

## Continuous Innovation

It is important to note that competition goes beyond the businesses and production that we see. Yes, those businesses compete. As we saw above, they compete both directly and indirectly by trying to buy the same inputs and trying to sell to the same customers. However, this is a much too limited view of competition that leaves out what is important in the longer term. Business do not only compete with existing businesses, but also compete with businesses that do not exist yet. And the businesses that exist are the outcome of such competition that already took place.

If this sounds strange, it is because we are used to looking at the economy as a state—a snapshot—and not as a process. Those businesses that exist today are the survivors of a competitive weeding out process that has already taken place. It is because these businesses were better—more productive, offered higher-quality goods, etc.—that they are currently *in* business. And they will stay in business only if they continue to be better than the competition. They need to outperform not merely the other surviving businesses, but also those businesses that have not yet been started or that are still developing or refining their products. This includes businesses producing goods that do not yet exist and may not even have been imagined yet but that could provide consumers with more value than the goods already available.

The innovation of new goods, production techniques, materials, organizations and so on fundamentally changes how an economy produces goods and what goods are produced. In the era when horse and buggy was the standard means of transportation, there was certainly competition between stables and transportation businesses just like there was competition between buggy manufacturers. But if we look only at those businesses, we could never explain how they were replaced and outcompeted by businesses that brought on the age of automobiles. Today, there are very few businesses profitably producing buggies. The reason is that automobiles provided consumers with greater value.

Seen from the perspective of consumers, horse buggies were valued goods *until there were affordable automobiles*. The automobiles provided greater value, which is why they undermined the profitability of and ultimately destroyed horse-and-buggy businesses. This is sometimes referred to as "creative destruction" that makes the core of economic development: older and less value-creative production gives way to new and more value-creative production.

When we recognize that this creative destruction is real and that it places constant pressure on businesses to innovate and reinvent themselves so as not to be replaced, we realize that it is impossible to understand the economy as anything other than a process. Economies evolve and unfold over time; they reinvent themselves. Competition is not merely the rivalry between two or more businesses producing and selling similar things, but the constant pressure to serve consumers better—both present and future. History is full of successful and influential businesses, many of them considered too big and "powerful" to compete with. Most of them are long gone and forgotten because someone figured out how to produce more value for consumers.

## CONTINUOUS UNCERTAINTY

Although the economy—and especially the *market* economy—is best understood as a process, it would be a mistake to think of it as a production process. We briefly addressed this above, but it is worth reiterating and elaborating on. An economy comprises production processes, but those production processes are themselves selected: they are the ones that survived the constant weeding out of less value-creative production. Many of those surviving production processes will, in turn, be weeded out as new and more value-creative ones are attempted.

A production process consists of the operations that make specific outputs from specific inputs. It is typically, but not necessarily, designed and organized. We can think of it as what happens within a factory. The exact operations that take place within the factory can change over time and so can the people and machines. Most of the parts are in some sense replaceable. Sometimes the factory itself is repurposed, but what makes it a factory is the same: it transforms inputs into outputs. The factory doesn't manufacture outputs in general—it is not a magical production machine. A factory produces clearly defined outputs (goods) using an engineered production process that requires specific inputs in certain quantities.

None of this applies to the economy as a process! The "output" of an economy is value in the form of consumer goods, but the actual goods produced change over time—and so do their respective value. The process of an economy is not its actual productions—the production processes and goods produced—but the continuous *selection* of those productions that provide the greatest value to consumers. Computers replaced typewriters and revolutionized office work flow, just as the automobile replaced the horse and buggy because it provided consumers with more highly valued transportation. Most all of our goods today, and the processes that produce them, will sooner or later be replaced by better, more valuable ones.

We cannot say which products will be attempted and even less which ones will be successful. Production, in other words, is always uncertain. It requires some form of investment before the value of the output can be known. This value is ultimately experienced by consumers when using goods, the expectation of which determines what price they are willing to pay. But it is not enough that goods satisfy wants—they have to do so, in the eyes of the consumer, to a greater degree than what he or she expects from other goods available. Only then will the consumer buy that product.

The number and variety of goods available depends on the imaginativeness of entrepreneurs and investors. In other words, the entrepreneur, who imagines, envisions, and aims to create new valued goods, drives the evolution of production in the economy. The consumer is then, after the fact, the judge of which entrepreneurs' productions are of sufficient value to be bought—and at what prices. The consumer, in other words, is sovereign and, through buying and not buying, determines which entrepreneurs earn profits and which entrepreneurs suffer losses.

CHAPTER 5

# Production and Entrepreneurship

Why do we produce? For the simple reason that nature doesn't automatically satisfy all of our needs and wants. Wild animals, grains, and berries are not enough to sustain the world population. Computers, airplanes, and hospitals do not grow on trees.

In other words, the means available to us are scarce. When we have more uses for something than we can possibly fulfill with what we have available, we must economize. That is, we need to make choices and consider the tradeoffs. It then makes sense to be careful in how resources are used so we don't waste them or use them for the wrong things.

There are two important strategies for dealing with scarcity. First, there is rationing, which means we limit our use of a resource so that it lasts longer. This is a common and appropriate strategy for any specific resource that is finite. For example, someone with only limited water and food—and no hope of gaining access to more—would benefit from restricting their drinking and eating to stay alive longer. However, this strategy, while intuitive, is typically inappropriate for society at large, and especially, markets.

The better strategy is production, which economizes *value*. Simply put, production allows us to satisfy more wants with the resources available—it creates more "bang" for the "buck" rather than only spreading out the "buck."

## PRODUCTION TO OVERCOME SCARCITY

Production alleviates the burden of scarcity by creating *better means*. It creates more value by changing, manipulating, and improving what nature provides. Because we engage in production, we can satisfy many more wants—and more highly valued wants—than would otherwise be possible.

The better we become at production, the more and better suited the means that are available to us. This is what "economic growth" means. The "larger" an economy is the more productive it is, which means it is better at satisfying consumer wants. It creates more value.[1]

Many consider bread to be a valued means of satisfying hunger. Whether or not we love bread, most of us find it more satisfying than munching on raw wheat and yeast and washing it down with water. Therefore we mix wheat flour and yeast together and make it into bread: the additional value of the bread justifies its production. We

---

[1] Note that this is not about creating stuff but *satisfying wants*. An economy that produces more goods does not necessarily produce more value than an economy that produces fewer goods. It could simply be more wasteful. What matters is the value of the goods produced, not their number or size—and certainly not the quantity of resources that were used to produce them. Production is the process of creating value; productivity is the measure of value produced per unit of input.

gain value even though it means that we use additional resources—oven, electricity, manpower—and must wait for the dough to rise and then bake.

It is easy to jump to conclusions and assume that the bread is valued more than the ingredients *because* additional resources were used to make it. This is false. It is the other way around: we choose to invest the resources—ingredients, manpower, time—because we expect the bread to give us greater satisfaction. By dedicating resources to making bread, including gaining the knowledge and expertise necessary to do it, the economy's capability to produce value increases. The investment makes us better off not only because we get bread, but because we gain the ability to bake bread. For as long as bread is a valued good and the ability to bake it is retained, the investment creates more value.

It is the expected value of the bread that makes the investment worth pursuing. If it were the case that something is worth more because we use more resources to produce it, then we are not actually economizing. Why use fewer resources if using *more* makes the good more valuable? We would then be better off the more resources we used. This is, of course, nonsense. We economize because using more resources than necessary is wasteful. We can produce more valuable output using those inputs if we avoid wasting them.

However, resource use and value output often correlate—they seem to go hand in hand, at least after the fact. The reason is that the expected value justifies the costs. In other words, if we aim to produce something that we expect to be of great value, then we can afford to use resources to produce it. In contrast, if we aim to produce a good that will be of only limited value, then we cannot justify using nearly as many resources. The costs are chosen based on the expected value that is being produced. This means that a premium or luxury product is not more expensive to buy because it is produced using rare, expensive materials—it was produced using rare, expensive materials *because the good is more expensive to buy*. Value determines cost, not the other way around.

This sounds backward, so let's illustrate by again considering making bread. Bread is a consumption good, so it is easy to understand it's value: it directly satisfies a want—it makes us better off because it satisfies hunger and tastes good. People may value bread differently, but they all value it for offering them some personal satisfaction. But what about the things that were needed to make the bread? The flour, yeast, water, oven, and electricity are not directly enjoyed by consumers but are merely means used to produce the final good. They only *in*directly satisfy consumers by making it possible to make bread.

These resources have value because they *contribute* to making bread. We can easily see this if we add resources that do not contribute to the consumer experience. Imagine if the baker buys a car engine and places it in the bakery. It's a cost to the bakery. But does it add value to the bread? The answer is: not at all. The engine does not increase the bread's value for consumers. Consumers do not value the bread higher and are not willing to pay a higher price for it just because the baker purchased an engine. Similarly with different types of flour or different ovens, which do contribute to the output. Consumers value the output, not the inputs. If they value wheat bread and rye bread equally, then it doesn't matter which flour the baker uses—so the cheaper would be the more economizing choice.

We can easily see this if we consider the opposite case. Imagine there is a baker and that people enjoy the bread this baker offers. Thus, the bread has value and so do the bakery and the ingredients the baker uses to make the bread. Now imagine that everyone suddenly stops wanting bread, so the baker can no longer sell it. What is the value of his bread? Zero. What would be the value of the baker's oven? The value of the oven falls too, perhaps to zero.

It is important to say "perhaps to zero," because it depends on what other uses bread ovens can be used for. If its use is only for making bread, then it no longer has a valued use. Why would anyone want a bread oven when nobody wants bread any longer? They wouldn't, so the oven is useless and has no value. But it may have scrap value if its materials (steel, glass, and so on) can be recycled and used for other purposes. The oven's value would then fall to the scrap value because that is now its highest-valued use.

This does not only apply to the oven's materials. If the oven can be used for something other than baking bread, then it might still have value higher than scrap. But the value *would* fall. Why? Because the reason it was used in baking and not something else is that baking was the higher-valued use. Indeed, the baker purchased or constructed the oven *because* it contributed to creating value. Economizing means we choose the higher-valued use because we get more value out of the resources. But this changes over time. If baking is no longer a valued use, the oven's value drops. Its value cannot be higher than its new best use in producing something else which is valued. If someone thinks of a better use for ovens than baking bread, then the oven is of higher value to that person than it is to the baker. We would then expect that person to, all else equal, offer and buy the oven from the baker at a price that is higher than the baker's valuation of it.

This simple example shows that the so-called means of production do not have value in themselves but only in terms of how they contribute to producing a valued consumer good. All productive resources have value *only* because they contribute to creating goods that consumers want. This is also true for something so distant from a consumer good as an oil tanker. Its value does not come from the resources used to make it but from how it is used in and contributes to valued production of consumer goods. And, of course, resources are used to make the oil tanker because it is expected to contribute to valued consumer goods. The expected value of the outcome that the oil tanker makes possible justifies the cost to produce it.

## Capital and Production

Production efforts are made to create goods for consumption, which directly satisfy wants, but not all production is of consumer goods. The oven used to bake bread is an example, as is the production of flour, yeast, and the bakery. The oven was constructed with the intention of *supporting* bread production. The oven, in other words, makes (or was at least intended to make) it easier to make bread and thus our productivity increases.

These "means of production" that only indirectly satisfy consumer wants are called *capital,* or *capital goods*. A consumer who buys bread does not care if the baker has an oven. Consumers generally care only about the consumer good and how well it satisfies their wants—not what or how much capital is used in the process of producing it.

But while his customers do not care, the baker certainly does. With the oven, more bread can be produced with less work. The effect of using capital is more output per unit of input, typically and especially labor, which means more wants can be satisfied using the same amount of resources. For the baker, this means more bread can be baked at lower cost. The purpose of capital and why it is used and created is that it increases our productivity. We get more valued output for the invested inputs.

Productivity is not only a matter of how much of something can be produced, but also what can be produced. Indeed, *economic* productivity is not a technological measure of units of output—it is a measure of *value*. Capital makes the production of certain types of goods possible, an often overlooked but very important role.

Let's revisit the baker again. Imagine that there is no oven, but that it is possible to bake flatbreads by placing the dough on a flat rock over an open fire. This baker spends his days baking flatbread this way. It is a worthwhile undertaking because flatbreads satisfy consumer wants better than the ingredients on their own. And there are enough consumers who prefer flat-bread to other types of simple bread that do not require ovens. In other words, baking flatbread is a productive use of the baker's labor, the flour, the rock, and the fire.

But an oven would make it possible for the baker to make new types of bread, which we (and, importantly, the baker) would expect to be of even greater value to consumers. Suppose a simple oven can be made from arranging flat rocks on top of the fire. Investing in gathering the rocks and arranging them in this way increases the value of the baker's bread-baking efforts. The rocks make an unsophisticated oven, but the baker can now produce other types of bread that consumers are expected to value more highly than flatbreads.

The rocks, arranged in this particular way, make a capital good: an oven. By spending time and effort to arrange the rocks over the fire, the baker has created new capital, that promises to increase the value for con-sumers. If things work out as planned, the result will be increased value output.

We often think of capital goods as durable. It is true that rocks last a long time, but this does not mean the oven will. In fact, use will eventually wear it down. For the oven to remain useful, repeated or continuous investments must be made to it, such as replacing bro-ken rocks. If this is not done, the usefulness of this capi-tal will fall over time and eventually lose its value as the oven becomes useless. We say that we "consume" capi-tal by using it. This applies to all capital but at different rates: some capital lasts longer and is more durable and may require less maintenance.

In addition to maintaining the oven itself, other supportive investments—such as keeping the fire going and grinding flour—must also be made to keep the capital useful. The whole capital structure requires continued investments. In fact, the oven is not useful unless the other capital necessary to produce bread is kept functional. All capital goods deteriorate with use and time. In other words, capital is added to increase productivity but is itself *used up* in producing consumer goods. We need constant reinvestments to keep capital useful and of value.

The oven made of rocks is of course not nearly as effective as our modern-day ovens. But it might be the best the baker can do at the time. To produce a longer-lasting and more effective oven, the baker would need access to steel and advanced tools that may not yet exist. Even if the baker figured out how such a modern oven could work, it may not be worth his time or effort to figure out how to turn rock into iron, iron into steel, and then make an oven out of it. He is a baker, after all. But someone else could do it. And someone else did, because today we do have modern, highly effective steel ovens.

Modern ovens are the result of centuries of investments in new and improved capital, refined designs, better materials, and more effective production technologies. We take this long and complex history for granted. But, this historical production cycle has led to the modern appliances that now are available in our neighborhood stores. The same is true for everything we can buy: every good is a refined piece of nature that was created for a single purpose—to provide us as consumers with want satisfaction.

All of those efforts that create materials, tools, machines, etc., are investments in capital that enhance production and allow us to satisfy more and more varied wants more effectively. Together, all this capital is arranged into a productive structure, that spans the whole economy, that allows us to effectively create a multitude of different goods that satisfy consumer wants.

We refer to the amount of capital, used in different combinations (such as the oven made from rocks and the fire) that allow society to produce distinct goods and services, as the economy's *capital structure*. This structure, as well as everything it comprises, was *created*. The production of new capital adds to the structure by adding or improving productive capabilities; maintenance investments extend existing capital's usefulness; and divestments and reallocations shift capital to the production of other goods, refining, adjusting, and changing the structure and thus the economy's productive capability. These actions, which bring about continuous change to the capital structure, are carried out by entrepreneurs.

## THE ROLE OF THE ENTREPRENEUR

Entrepreneurs are in the business of creating our future. They do this by creating new goods or refining and improving  production. In both cases, they bring about changes to the capital structure by either changing the use of existing capital or creating new capital. The aim in both is to create more value for consumers. If they are successful entreprenedurs get paid in *profits*.

However, *time* and *risk* play an important role in this process.

Like the baker, who created a simple oven out of rocks and thereby could provide consumers with new types of bread, entrepreneurs imagine and bet that they can better satisfy consumers. This means they make investments to change things, seeking to create more value by increasing value productivity. They produce goods because they believe those goods will better serve consumers and, therefore, will be in great demand. When such an investment is successful, consumers get more value at lower cost, part of which entrepreneurs keep as profit. When it fails, which means consumers do not approve of what entrepreneurs offer, the investment loses value and may be lost completely.

The major problem entrepreneurs face is that the value of production effort is not known until it is completed. It is only when the finished good is sold that the entrepreneur learns if the investment was worthwhile—if consumers want the good. In contrast, costs are known and incurred long before the good is completed and offered for sale. Note that these costs are not merely the inputs that make the output, such as the flour, yeast, and water that are turned into bread, but also the capital needed: the oven, the bakery, etc. Even in those cases when an entrepreneur takes orders and is paid before producing the actual good, some costs are incurred as part of the not-yet-produced good. Those costs include such things as setting up the business, experimenting with capital, figuring out how to make an oven, developing a recipe or blueprint for production. Investments must be made to produce the good, which can then be sold.

This problem is often referred to as *uncertainty bearing*. Entrepreneurship is the economic function of bearing the uncertainty of creating future goods: production without knowledge of whether it is value creative and profitable or will it incur a loss. It is the potential for profit that justifies undertaking production and bearing the uncertainty of entrepreneurial investment. It is the possibility of suffering losses that moderates those efforts and forces entrepreneurs to be responsive to consumer wants. And entrepreneurs must be responsive, because consumers are sovereign in their choices to purchase and use goods, which means only consumers determine the value of goods.

Because the value of any good is unknown—*cannot* be known—before it is used, entrepreneurs invest in production based on what they imagine consumers will value. The baker created the oven because he imagined the new types of bread would serve consumers better. The higher expected value justified the cost of developing and building the oven. By undertaking this endeavor, the baker changed what is and can be produced in the economy. Indeed, the actions of entrepreneurs direct overall production by refining and adjusting the economy's capital structure. In establishing productive capability and determining what goods can and will be produced, entrepreneurship *drives* the market process. All goods produced and made available to us, whether they end up successful and profitable or not, are the results of entrepreneurial undertakings—entrepreneurs' uncertainty bearing.

However, while this is the outcome and implication of their efforts, individual entrepreneurs are not in the business of adjusting the capital structure for overall efficiency or the social good. Entrepreneurs invest in particular productive capabilities in pursuit of profits. But it is very difficult to figure out what consumers will find valuable, which means entrepreneurship is fraught with failure. The entrepreneurs' task is in fact made even more difficult in markets where it is not enough to produce something valuable, but they must outdo each other in terms of value. Entrepreneurs compete to serve consumers in the best possible way.

## Entrepreneurs Make Mistakes

The future is very difficult to predict, but this is what entrepreneurs attempt to do: they invest in creating the future in hope that consumers will find it valuable. And they do so while competing with the visions of other entrepreneurs. So it should be no surprise that there is an extremely high rate of failure.

This may seem inefficient or wasteful, but it is not. It would be *if what consumers value were known*, because with such knowledge of the future, production can be easily streamlined for efficiency. Entrepreneurship, however, solves another problem. Value is in the minds of consumers—it is not known beforehand, but consumers experience it when they use a good to satisfy wants.

Very often, consumers do not themselves know how to best satisfy their wants. Instead, entrepreneurs imagine a good they think, based on their own ingenuity, experience, and understanding, will serve consumers. To provide greater value than the goods already offered for sale, and therefore have a chance to earn profits, entrepreneurs must step ahead of consumers and introduce to them a valuable solution that they perhaps had not considered. As Henry Ford is thought to have said: "If I had asked people what they wanted, they would have said faster horses."[2] Indeed, most people probably thought they simply wanted faster horses, but Ford imagined that horseless buggies would offer higher value to consumers—and he was able to offer automobiles at prices that consumers would buy.

The fact is that consumers, whether or not they can say what goods they want, always choose between the goods offered to them. That's when consumers exercise their sovereignty: entrepreneurs cannot force consumers to buy anything, they can only produce goods that consumers value and therefore choose.

The calculus for a consumer is simple but difficult for entrepreneurs to foresee and meet. First, the good has to offer value by satisfying some want that the consumer has. If what the entrepreneur offers has no value to the consumer, then it is not a good.

Second, the good must offer a better, more valuable means to satisfy a want than other goods offering to satisfy that same want. If it does not, then the good is ineffective and of lesser value for satisfying that want. Consequently, the entrepreneur must offer it at a lower price to make it worthwhile to the consumer.

Third, the good must offer value that exceeds the goods that promise to satisfy *other* wants. Entrepreneurs compete for the consumers' money.

---

[2]This quote is oft repeated and makes a vital point about entrepreneurship and production, but it is doubtful that Ford actually said this.

Fourth, the good must offer enough value for the consumer to buy it now rather than choose to hold on to their money and buy something else in the future.

The entrepreneur must provide value in accordance with *all* of these layers of consumer valuation.

Needless to say, entrepreneurs attempt to do something extremely difficult. They do so because they believe they will profit in some way in the end. But whether or not they do, their attempts to create value provide a crucial service to other entrepreneurs and the economy overall (we will discuss economic calculation in chapter 7). As they compete based on their own knowledge and imaginations—how they expect to best be of service to consumers—they create knowledge for the economy overall. Entrepreneurs' discoveries of what consumers value, identified by profits, guide new entrepreneurs in their efforts. Similarly with losses, which suggest to other entrepreneurs that they should try something different. Consequently, every attempted entrepreneurial undertaking can take advantage of the knowledge and experiences of previous entrepreneurs. This makes entrepreneurial value production cumulative: successes are augmented and become stepping stones for future production; errors are weeded out.

It would be wrong to disparage failing entrepreneurs, however. Even though they were unsuccessful and suffer losses, they provided the economy with an invaluable service by making information available on what does not work. This is valuable information for all other entrepreneurs. As entrepreneurs fail, the resources—capital—that they invested become available to other entrepreneurs, who can then increase their own production or try something new.

In sum, *entrepreneurs serve consumers by creating our future*. They do this by trying ideas for new, imagined goods and, based on their expected value, paying wages to workers and developing new capital. When entrepreneurs err in their choices, they personally suffer the loss of those investments. That loss is the totality of the investments they made in production: wages paid to employees and prices paid to capital suppliers.

CHAPTER 6

# Value, Money, and Price

So far, our discussion about the economy has been exclusively from the perspective of *value*. Value is the ultimate goal of our actions and what motivates our behavior. It is personal—*subjective* which means it comes from satisfying a want. If we are hungry, we consume food; if we feel lonely, we might visit a friend.

Value is the removal of or fulfillment of some uneasiness (hunger or loneliness), which makes us better off. We can compare satisfactions, for example, that we like oranges more than apples and we like pears more than either. Simple value comparisons in terms of our own personal satisfactions are unproblematic. If we are both hungry and thirsty, we can quickly decide which uneasinesses to remove first by considering how urgently we feel each one. But although we can make comparisons and determine which satisfaction would be greater, there are no *units* of value.

## THE PROBLEM OF MEASURING VALUE

We cannot measure the extent to which we removed uneasiness by taking a certain action. The satisfaction this brings is a feeling we experience, which has no units or exact measures. We cannot say that we like oranges 2.5 times more than apples and pears 1.3 times more than oranges.

We cannot compare the subjective values of different people, as their experienced satisfactions are personal. It is nonsense to say that Adam likes pears 20 percent more than Beth likes pears. Perhaps Adam exclaims that he likes pears "a lot," whereas Beth doesn't care for them at all. If that is how they truly feel, then Beth might offer to give Adam her pear. But this is still *not* a measure of how much they each value pears, nor is it a comparison using some universal unit of satisfaction. Beth values giving Adam the pear, perhaps her feelings for Adam are strong and she knows he likes pears. But it doesn't tell us anything about *how much* Beth—or Adam—values keeping or giving away the pear.

The lack of measure makes value problematic in a social setting—especially in advanced economies with long, specialized production processes (which we will discuss in chapter 7). How do we economize on scarce resources so that we get as much value as possible?

To illustrate, imagine a small society of 150 people where there is enough water to quench the thirst of forty-five individuals and food to satisfy thirty of them. How do you determine which forty-five are "most thirsty" and which thirty are "most hungry"?[1]

---

[1]To be formally accurate, we should ask who would experience the greatest satisfaction from drinking or eating (removing the uneasiness of thirst and hunger, respectively).

This society could decide to use the water and food to invest in production, which could allow them to create even more value. If ten people are provided enough water and food to last them three days, then they can go get more water and food and bring it back to the others. Should this society make this investment? Should they send one party of ten or two parties of five out in different directions to search? Whom should they choose to collect the newly obtained water and food? Who among the remaining population should get whatever water and food remains? Such comparisons require some measure of value, but because value is a personal experience, there isn't one. There is no solution to this economization problem.

Markets solve this conundrum by using money and prices, which provide objective social relative valuations (more on this below) and therefore allow for comparisons and economizing in terms of valued goods. If pears cost us 1.3 times as much as oranges, we can easily decide how to use our purchasing power to get as much satisfaction as possible: buy pears, buy oranges, or buy some combination of both. We can make such comparisons individually as well as collaboratively. As we will see, money and prices are indispensable for an economy. We cannot function without them.

## THE USE OF MONEY

We tend to take both money and prices for granted. They are so universally present that most think of money as a measure of value. They even think of value itself in terms of money. This is a mistake.

Money is the *commonly used medium of exchange,* and it has value to us because it provides this function. We value money like other goods, because of what it can do for us. But it is not the bills and coins themselves that provide us with value, but the expectation that we can use them to buy what we want. This means money works because we recognize it as such and therefore accept it in exchange. Money has *purchasing power*. It is the belief that money can buy goods that makes it valuable. If we believed that we would not be able to use money to buy goods—perhaps we believe others will not accept it—then we too would not accept it.

This means money is money because people consider it to be money. In this sense, money is a largely self-reinforcing social institution. We all have experience using it and thus have some idea of what it means for something to be money. But this does not explain what money is, why it is, or how it came to be.

Consider what would make you accept something as money. Or, to get to the real issue: what would make a society that does not use money accept something as money. Because money's value is that others will accept it in exchange, nothing that aspires to be money will have value as money to begin with. Only after a thing has been broadly adopted in exchange will something be recognized as money—but not before.

This leads many to assert that money must have been imposed from the top down by decree to use it in exchanges. The idea is that some head of state invented the concept of money and introduced it to facilitate trade (or, perhaps, payment of taxes). But this "explanation" misses the point: unless something is already a money, people will not voluntarily accept it in exchange. So it has no or little value before it is deemed money.

A decree does not create a money—it creates only an obligation, which is limited by the extent of its enforcement. However, it is fully conceivable that a government can, bit by bit, take over and monopolize an already existing money, which we have seen happen. Most currencies today are government monopoly monies, but that is not how money was invented or accepted as a medium of exchange—it is only how it ended up. The *economic function* of money cannot simply be created from the top down.

People choose to exchange goods for their own benefit, which means voluntary exchange must be for the parties' mutual benefit. Both expect to become better off or they wouldn't choose to exchange. An obligation to accept something that is not directly valuable to them—such as an imposed currency not yet accepted as money—would lessen people's willingness to trade. After all, if you were compelled to accept rocks in "payment" for your belongings, then you probably would refrain from offering them up for sale. Even if I offered you a ton of rocks, you would not exchange them for your house or car. Why trade a valued good for something you don't want? So even if you were required to pay your taxes using rocks, you would limit your trade for rocks to fulfill that duty—but not more. The market for exchanging goods for rocks would be very limited.

Such exchanges would happen by choice only if the payment offered were actual money. In a society where there is no money, people not only lack trust in the money's purchasing power—they have no understanding of the concept itself. Imagine offering a stack of dollar bills or a gold coin to a person from the Stone Age in exchange for their axe or food.

## The Emergence of Money

Money is an economic concept. Dollar bills aren't money in themselves, but money can exist in the form of dollar bills. However, those bills are money only because and for as long as they are accepted as such. This becomes obvious when we travel to other countries because what is money in one country may not be accepted as money in another. You cannot use Swedish kronor for payment in Austria or the United States, even though everyone in Sweden accepts them as money.

We know very little about the historical origins of money, but the concept is clear. The economist Carl Menger showed how a barter economy can transition into a money economy.[2] Menger's explanation requires no central planner or decree—money *emerges*. This is important because it provides insight into the meaning and role of money *as an economic concept*.

In a barter economy, people trade goods for goods. This economy suffers from obvious limitations, because each exchange requires that both parties get something they want in a quantity they want, without using anything we call money. In other words, someone who offers eggs for sale and wishes to buy butter needs to

---

[2]Carl Menger, "On the Origin of Money," trans. Caroline A. Foley, *Economic Journal* 2, no. 6 (June 1892): 239–55.

find someone who is selling butter and wants eggs in exchange. This greatly limits the number of potential trading partners.

Because goods differ in durability and size, barter economies could not develop into productive economies with division of labor. Consider a boat builder who wants to sell his newly designed speedboat. Even if he would want eggs, he would hardly accept thousands of eggs in exchange—they would go bad and be useless in a short period of time. So he would need to find someone offering the exact bundle of goods that he wants and is willing to sell for the boat. The parties also need to agree on the rates: How many eggs for the boat?

People exchange goods to become better off, that is they trade *for value.* Menger noted that people will seek any number of ways to get around the limitations of barter. If the dairy farmer is not willing to accept my eggs for butter but I know he will accept bread, then I can approach the baker to exchange eggs for bread—and if the baker agrees, I can then exchange the bread for butter. In other words, I exchange eggs for bread not because I want bread but because I want to use the bread to obtain butter. My first exchange facilitates the second, from which I benefit directly.

If I wanted berries, for example, I would have to go through the same procedure if the person offering berries does not want my eggs but would accept something else. I would sell my eggs for that something else in order to exchange it for berries. Even though the eggs work in some cases, they won't work in all. But let's say some of them accept the same different good in exchange for bread. Knowing this, I could exchange my eggs for bread simply because I believe the bread will be more useful when I go on my next grocery run. In Menger's terms, I sell my eggs to acquire a *more saleable good*, for the sole purpose of using it in exchange; to me it serves only the indirect purpose of facilitating the actual exchanges. Thus, it makes sense for me to acquire bread even if I don't fancy it—and even if I am allergic to it.

As people exchange their products for more saleable goods, the more saleable goods become more sought after *because they can be used to buy many goods*. And as more people realize how useful these goods are as facilitators of exchange, more people sell their own goods (I my eggs, the dairy farmer her butter, etc.) for those more saleable goods. Eventually, by people's actions but not by their design, one or a few goods emerge as commonly used media of exchange—monies. They are valued primarily as media of exchange, not for being goods in themselves.

## The Importance of Money

In a money economy, we use money to pay for goods and can easily compare prices because they are all expressed in the same unit—a currency. But, as we've seen in previous chapters, prices are really exchange ratios. Money serves as an intermediary that facilitates trade that elevates us above the limitations of barter trade.

The existence of money uncouples people's buying and selling in terms of goods. It makes universal purchasing power of the exchange value of goods. In other words, I can sell my goods or services to one person but use the purchasing power gained in return (as money) to buy goods or services from someone else. This seems obvious because we are used to it. However, the implications are enormous.

Under barter trade, employment would be possible only where an employer can offer the specific goods an employee will accept as payment. Imagine that your employers paid for labor not in money but instead in specific food items: clothing, hygiene products, books, travel, furniture, etc. It is easy to see that finding an employer who offers the most desirable bundle of goods would be almost impossible. It would likely mean that you would need to accept a bundle that is far from perfect to gain employment. You could do much better if you received the exchange value of those goods instead—the purchasing power (money)—and used it to buy the goods you prefer.

Money is therefore much more than a convenience—it is necessary for exchanges to take place and for the advanced, specialized production processes we take for granted in the modern economy. Large-scale production, supply chains, and specialization are made possible because money uncouples our efforts as both buyers and sellers. Due to the uncoupling, we can also specialize in what we do well rather than produce only what we ourselves want to consume. Consequently, we can focus our production efforts on where we make the biggest difference—where we create most value *for society*. Without money, we would not be nearly as productive.

The uncoupling also means we can use our acquired purchasing power—what we are paid for producing—on what we find most valuable. Money makes it possible for us to pursue wants that would never be within reach with barter. The consequence of having and using money means not only greatly improved production but also that we can pursue more valuable consumption. The former facilitates and increases the opportunities for the latter. And the more value we produce, the more purchasing power we are paid in return.

Because all actors in a money economy can pursue those goods they value most—and can produce those goods that others highly value—there is more value overall. We are much better off in a money economy than in a barter economy.

## Money Prices

Money makes prices easy to compare. Rather than expressing prices as ratios—where each good is "priced" in terms of all other goods—they are expressed in money.

In a barter economy, my buying bread with eggs in order to buy butter requires that the three parties establish exchange ratios. I might be able to exchange a dozen eggs for three slices of bread from the baker. In this transaction, the price of one slice of bread is four eggs and the price of one egg is a quarter slice of bread. I can then use the bread to purchase a pound of butter for two slices of bread, making the bread price of butter two slices per pound and the butter price of bread half a pound per slice.

I am party to both transactions and can infer that the "price" of one pound of butter is eight eggs. That is a simplification, because the dairy farmer does not accept eggs in exchange. The problem is that the prices of all goods here are expressed as ratios of all other goods. If, for example, the dairy farmer would also accept eight cups of berries for a pound of butter, then the price of one pound of butter would be *either* two slices of bread *or* eight cups of berries. Such ratios (prices *in kind*) could be established for all combinations of goods in any possible exchange. But how can we compare them? Without a common denominator, these prices are all unique exchange ratios that is difficult to keep straight or make sense of.

Let us assume that bread emerges as money in the example above. This means that bread, serving as the medium of exchange, becomes one side of virtually every transaction. In other words, the prices of all goods can be expressed in terms of bread—because they are traded for bread. So, I would sell my eggs for bread and use bread to buy butter and berries. As bread is the common denominator, I can easily compare prices and buy the good that will best satisfy my wants. Now, because bread is money, all sellers of goods are likely to accept it as payment because they want the purchasing power, not the bread itself.

If a pound of butter costs two slices of bread and a slice of bread buys two cups of berries, then it is easy for me to compare prices. The three slices of bread that I was paid for my dozen eggs can buy either one-and-a-half pounds of butter, six cups of berries, or some other combination. All I need to do now is determine which option I value more highly. I can easily calculate how to get most value for each slice of bread.

In this money economy, all goods are priced in terms of bread, and bread is priced in terms of all goods. As bread is the medium of exchange, we can say that the purchasing power of (a slice of) bread is half a pound of butter, two cups of berries, four eggs, etc. Consequently, it is much easier for everyone in society to determine whether something is "worth it."

Another way to say this is that the opportunity cost of buying two cups of berries for a slice of bread is the value of whatever else one can buy for that slice of bread: half a pound of butter, four eggs, and so on. Obviously, we would choose to buy whatever available good we expect will provide us with the greatest satisfaction. As everybody strives for value—and, thanks to money, can properly compare prices—our actions produce implicit bidding for the goods that have been produced. Our willingness and ability to buy a good at a certain price constitutes our *demand*.

The highest bidder for a good will receive it first and will not have to do without. Those who bid less money for the good will be served later until the sellers no longer think the bread offered is worth it. The more people value a good, the higher its market price. And the more of the good is for sale, the lower its market price.

Similarly, because our buying and selling efforts are uncoupled, we can produce what will get us the most money in return. We now can expend our labor where we have greater skill and expertise and where we can get the highest payment in money. What this means is that to benefit ourselves (higher payment), we choose to contribute to the economy in the way that consumers value most highly. In a market setting, the purchasing power that we are offered in return for our services tend to be proportionate to the value we contribute to the market in money prices.

As a result, the free market provides those who contribute most value in production with the most purchasing power, which means they in turn also have a greater ability to satisfy their own wants by buying their preferred goods and services. Purchasing power—and therefore consumption power—the extent to which people are able to satisfy their wants through goods—is consequently a reflection of one's contribution to the economy (as a producer). Simply put, what we supply constitutes our ability to demand.

## Fiat Currency and Price Inflation

The discussion above explained the *economic concept* of money as commodity money. Historically speaking, different things were money in different societies: rocks, seashells, cattle, etc. In Europe and beyond, gold and silver emerged as universal, international money.

The paper money we use today is an evolution of precious metal coins and banking. The process is as follows. Banks sell space in their vaults for safe-keeping of people's money. Money is fungible, meaning it does not matter if you get the same gold or silver coin back from the bank, so banks can keep all customers' coins in the same vault and issue receipts for the number of coins each customer has on deposit. As those receipts are redeemable in coins, people can use them in exchange directly instead of having to take them to the bank first. Those who end up with a receipt can deposit it with their own bank, which in turn makes a claim on the bank that issued the receipt. At regular intervals, the banks clear all their claims by transporting the net gold and silver owed, saving everybody a lot of trouble.

This practice has a downside: it offers banks an incentive to issue more receipts than there is money in their vault. As receipts are not all redeemed at the same time and money is fungible, this practice can provide banks with unearned purchasing power.

In a free-banking system, such abuse would arguably be kept at a lower level. A bank would only be able to issue these additional "cash" receipts as long as the practice is not discovered and the bank is able to maintains its reputation. But as soon as holders of those receipts were not sure if the bank had sufficient money in its vaults—is the bank insolvent—they would act to redeem their receipts. Historically, there are many examples of banks losing their reputations and their customers flocking to withdraw their money, causing a bank run. If the bank has issued more receipts than it can redeem in money, the run bankrupts it.

A bank's insolvency due to over issue of paper money can also be discovered in banks' clearing of claims. A clearinghouse establishes the banks' balances and calculates what money should be transported from one bank to another to balance the accounts. If a bank issues too much paper money, this will be discovered during the clearing of transactions because the other banks have receipts from this bank and demand that it transport real money to them—money that it may not have. So the over issue of paper receipts can be discovered both by customers and by competing banks. The risk of getting caught, which means bankruptcy, is substantial.

In modern times, most monies are national monopoly currencies issued by the government's central bank and have no backing, as the receipts in our example did. This turn of events is explained partly as government's attempt to solve the problem of bank runs and partly by its aim to exploit the power of issuing money. As the monopoly issuer of money, the government/ central bank can provide itself with purchasing power at no apparent cost.

However, as we saw above, a money's purchasing power is expressed in the relationship between the money and the goods available. As the new money is used to buy goods on the market, prices are bid up beyond where they otherwise would be because there is more money in circulation. When this happens we see a general, but not uniform, increase in prices when new money enters the market. This is price inflation.

Fiat currency—created by the government's legal monopolization of money—tends to be inflationary. It is easier for the government to provide itself with purchasing power through the printing press than to tax people. However, the effect is that the purchasing power of money falls, which makes people comparatively poorer and distorts the capital structure (as we saw in chapter 3). This type of money-driven distortion wreaks havoc on the economy, as we will see in the next chapter, and ultimately causes the boom-bust cycle (discussed in chapter 8).

CHAPTER 7

# Economic Calculation

Money, as we discussed in the previous chapter, makes lots of exchanges possible that are impractical or impossible under barter trade. We are better off as a result. But money has greater implications that are often overlooked or misunderstood. Chief among these is *economic calculation*, which is the process of determining how scarce resources should be used to produce the most valuable outcomes possible. Economic calculation is a core of any economy.

We can use technological knowledge to maximize a production process' outcomes, given the inputs and outputs, and to reject inputs that are unsuitable for that type of production. But which input to use, which production process to undertake, which production technologies produce the better (higher-value) outcome, and which outcomes to strive for are fundamentally economic decisions.

For example, technological knowledge can tell us that gold is too soft to use for railroad tracks. But it cannot tell us which harder metal is best—most valuable—to use: iron, steel, or platinum? The answer requires knowing what else those metals can be used for, how valuable those uses are, and how much of each metal is available. Technological knowledge also cannot tell us when, how, or whether to build the railroad. Where should the railroad be built? Should it be built at all or should the resources go to building some other type of infrastructure—or something else altogether? Those are all economic questions—they are based on our calculation of the relative *value* outcome.

A metal that is far from technologically perfect may actually be the best choice, even if it means laying new rails from time to time. The best solution in terms of technology gives us little to no information on the value outcome of the cost of production. Without economic calculation, an economy is unable to economize on scarce resources.

Money facilitates economic calculation, an essential mechanism in a market economy, by serving as a common unit. In other words, it allows for *monetary calculation*.

## The Nature of a Productive Economy

Economists have long known that productivity is closely related to specialization. We saw in chapter 5 that capital increases productivity and it does so by making labor more productive. We get more out of our labor efforts if we use appropriate tools and machines. Market exchange also makes labor more productive because people can focus on producing the things that create most value regardless of whether they personally value or use them. Instead of people being self-sufficient and producing everything they need for their everyday lives, markets allow them to develop their unique abilities and take advantage of economies of scale—of how average cost falls with higher production volumes—to increase their overall value output.

Specialization, or focusing our time and effort on a narrower set of productive activities, has two main effects.

First, when we specialize, we become better at carrying out specific productive activities. Adam Smith noted that specializing makes us many times more effective and productive because we (1) do not lose time shifting from one task to another, (2) develop and increase dexterity and workmanship, and (3) can more easily identify how to use simple machines or develop new tools to become even more effective.

Smith exemplified this "division of labor" with a pin factory in which the production of a pin takes eighteen distinct operations. In Smith's example, "a workman ... could scarce, perhaps, with his utmost industry, make one pin in a day, and certainly could not make twenty." But if ten workmen instead specialize in carrying out certain operations, they "could make among them upwards of forty-eight thousand pins in a day." That's an enormous difference—specializing increases the output of labor at least *twenty-four hundred times*.

The difference is not in the tools or operations, which are the same in both cases but in better organization of the production process. Or, specialization allows workers to be much more productive.

Second, when we specialize—and *because* we specialize—we become dependent on others doing their part of the production process—and they on us. The serial division of labor in a production process creates interdependence: the ten workmen in Smith's example can produce an enormous number of pins together, but only as long as all of them carry out their tasks. If one worker, who is in the middle of the production process, does not show up for work, this creates a gap in the process. The workers in the earlier operations up to the point where the missing worker's task begins will be able to do their part, but the workers requiring the input from the missing worker cannot carry out their operations, and so no pins will be produced. For the process to generate any pins at all, all tasks must be carried out. Simply put, the ten specialized workers stand and fall together. If the chain is broken, for whatever reason, they will revert from producing forty-eight thousand pins to a measly two hundred (the max for ten unspecialized workers in Smith's example).

Such interdependence is risky and might sound like a bad idea, but it is not. Each of these workers has an interest in completing the process; otherwise there would be no pins to sell and no job. (As an unspecialized worker they could make no more than twenty pins each and have a lower standard of living.) So because their specialized productive efforts are interdependent, the workers share an interest in completing the production process.

Smith's argument is more general and not just limited to factory production. The capital structure itself is the outcome of specialization: a division of resources that facilitates, strengthens, and enhances the division of labor.

When the flatbread baker builds an oven (see chapter 5), he not only increases his productivity as a baker but also develops the knowledge and skill to produce ovens. If there are other bakers interested in using his innovation, our baker could specialize in oven making instead of baking. He could supply other bakers, who can then specialize in producing oven-baked bread. The baker's role has changed from baking bread to supplying ovens and his livelihood now depends on the availability of the resources needed to produce ovens and then sell them. It is an opportunity to create more value and increase his—and everybody else's—living standards.

This simple example of the baker shows how a longer production process, through innovations and the resultant intensive division of labor and capital, is adopted because it produces more value. It is more productive than using scarce resources, especially labor, more effectively. The modern economy has extremely long production processes with such narrow specializations that most of us would not be able to survive without the rest of the economy. Think about everything you rely on and use in your daily life but that you did not produce yourself—and probably *cannot* produce. We depend on a lot of strangers doing their part in production.

On the flip side, an economy could never sustain the many people that live in the world today without specialization. And the smaller population it could support would not have the conveniences and number of goods available to us. Our modern prosperity is the result of the division of labor and capital, which is constantly enhanced and improved through innovation and competition in the market.

The market reduces the risks and potential downsides of interdependence in production and supply chains by influencing parallel production processes—redundancy. When a new and specialized production process earns profits, it will quickly be copied by entrepreneurs eager to share that profit. In other words, if the oven-maker earns high profits from his ovens, others will attempt to do the same. They will develop parallel production structures to capture a share of the market.

With this type of imitative competition, the risk that production will not be completed is greatly diminished. Imagine if the oven-maker had employed several workers to build the ovens through a specialized production process. The success of the whole undertaking depends on all of the workers doing their part. But when others imitate this process to capture some of the profits in the oven industry, they can use and complete a half-finished oven that another entrepreneur could not complete. Thus, failure due to interdependence is of little concern in markets, in contrast to centralized processes.

Is redundancy inefficient? Why have many producers offering the same goods instead of one factory producing on a larger scale? This overlooks the fact that the market is a process (more on this below)—that one firm is not enough to establish all the highly specialized processes. There are two main reasons for this. First, incompleteness: those highly specialized and unique processes would be high-risk because every specialized task would make or break them. It is not obvious that using economies of scale provides more benefits than lacking redundancy which also risks the whole process failing. Second, refinement: innovations in production are never perfect from the beginning but become better through competition, as new entrepreneurs figure out how to improve function. Without the market's redundancy, we would never get production processes good enough to build economies of scale.

The second point requires some elaboration. Much refinement and progress happen as market competition divides production processes into ever smaller, more specialized tasks and processes. Entrepreneurs constantly try to outdo existing production by innovating and finding better ways of production. They replace parts of the existing processes with more highly specialized subprocesses that are expected to be more productive and could provide a competitive advantage. Entrepreneurs' profit-driven innovation increasingly subdivides and decentralizes production procesesses. What used to be specialized parts of a novel production process become standardized capital goods and services traded in the market.

Consider this example. Early on, entrepreneurs implemented new ideas to keep track of and manage production, as well as to increase sales. These ideas expanded into accounting and marketing departments, whose specializations made these tasks more productive. Today accounting and marketing are separate businesses because entrepreneurs discovered that it was more productive to specialize in one or the other and sell these services to businesses as separate entities. This lets producers focus on production, accountants on accounting, and marketers on marketing. They can each specialize in their trade, improve their respective processes, and increase their overall output. It is the same reason that farmers do not build their own tractors, do not develop their own seeds, nor make their own fertilizers and pesticides.

Productive interdependence also comes with a positive *social* outcome. We noted in the previous discussion that our ability to demand—our purchasing power—comes from producing value for others. As the economy becomes ever more specialized, our personal contribution increasingly depends on the productive contributions of others. And vice versa. This also means that I, in this market setting, must serve others to serve myself, because my ability to demand is based on the value of my supply. Consequently, the more I interact with, learn about, and understand others, the better I can produce what they value most. This applies both to self-employed entrepreneurs, who seek to serve their customers and to employees in large corporations, who are paid wages for how well they serve their employers. Thus, market production is empathic—your ability to provide value *for others* ultimately determines the value you get in return for your efforts.

This means the market process is not only about production but is a civilizing process: it requires and augments social cooperation for our mutual and common benefit. There are no contradictions in open market production—there is only value and the pursuit of it through empathic production. Competition is in fact cooperation: it is not directed or designed but acted out through the price mechanism. And with it comes a better understanding and respect for other people's points of view—because this makes us better.

Ludwig von Mises was very clear:

Society is the outcome of conscious and purposeful behavior. This does not mean that individuals have concluded contracts by virtue of which they have founded human society. The actions which have brought about social cooperation and daily bring it about anew do not aim at anything else than cooperation and coadjuvancy with others for the attainment of definite singular ends. The total complex of the mutual relations created by such concerted actions is called society. It substitutes collaboration for the—at least conceivable—isolated life of individuals. Society is division of labor and combination of labor. In his capacity as an acting animal man becomes a social animal.[1]

The economy and society are two sides of the same coin. It is not possible to separate the market process from society and civilization.

## The Driving Force

We have referred to the market economy as a process but have not yet discussed what makes it a process.

The market that we interact with and can observe is actually a number of production processes that generate the goods and services we can buy. These processes

---

[1]See Ludwig von Mises, *Human Action: A Treatise on Economics*, scholar's ed. (Auburn, AL: Ludwig von Mises Institute, 1998), p. 143.

generate jobs that allow us to earn an income and with that income we can choose to buy goods.

But the market process is not merely the production of goods that is currently underway. Who decides what new goods should be produced? The simple answer is entrepreneurs. They think of new goods and new production processes that they think will benefit consumers and therefore earn them a profit. But entrepreneurs cannot know that what they produce and offer for sale will be fancied—or at what prices consumers are willing to spend. So entrepreneurs speculate—they bet that what they imagine is valuable will be valued by consumers. By doing this, entrepreneurs drive the market process forward. They constantly challenge the status quo in their quest for creating more value.

Entrepreneurs attempt to create new value and drive the evolution of production in the long term. For example, in the year 1900, the production of personal transportation centered around making horses and buggies available. But in the year 2000, it was about manufacturing automobiles. This change is what the market process is: constant change and refinement of what and how it is produced.

Entrepreneurship is the driving force of the market process. The great shift from horse and buggy to automobiles was a matter of entrepreneurial innovation, part of what economist Joseph A. Schumpeter famously called "creative destruction." The creative aspect of the shift was the appearance of the automobile—a new type of personal transportation offered to consumers. Specifically, it was the introduction of Henry Ford's Model T—an affordable, mass-produced automobile—that made the new automobiles accessible to so many consumers. People didn't choose to do away with horses and buggies but rather chose automobilites because they provided more value. Therein lies the "destruction"—the market for horse-and-buggy transportation collapsed because consumers received greater value elsewhere.

To put this in different terms, automobiles provided greater value to consumers than their previously preferred means of transportation. Consequently, the people who had bred and trained horses and built buggies were no longer contributing sufficient value. Their businesses and professions were therefore soon replaced by ones that consumers valued more.

Businesses and professions that had emerged in support of horse-and-buggy transportation either disappeared or had to evolve into the production of other goods. So, today we have only a few stables but there are many iron mines, steel plants, and gas stations to support the automobile.

These shifts toward new value constantly occur in the market. Sometimes we are aware of them because they are swift and affect us personally. But often we are unaware of the changes. The latter is typically the case when major changes occur *within* production processes but do not affect consumers' goods. The computer, for example, revolutionized both production processes and how firms operated. Although computers can make a production process more efficient—or completely restructure it—consumers often do not notice the difference in the goods offered in stores. But producers see it as new professions and specializations begin to appear. These new value-creating jobs offer higher wages and new types of careers. There were no computer professionals in 1900, but it was a common and respected career in 2000—and they earned a much higher standard of living than the most skilled carpenters producing top-of-the-line buggies in 1900.

## THE PRODUCTION OF VALUE

Entrepreneurs compete with both existing businesses and other entrepreneurs to produce new value for consumers. Entrepreneurs have a more important role. In speculating and betting on new value creation, entrepreneurs provide the means for economic calculation—they determine the money prices of the means of production. This is fundamentally important—it is what makes the economy possible. Without entrepreneurs providing this function, it would be impossible to economize resources and discover new innovative production processes.

To understand this we need to consider what entrepreneurs do. Specifically, we must consider what their actions as a whole mean. As with so many things in the economy, observable phenomena emerge from people's actions but are not created by any one person. Instead, they are patterns (order) that emerge from people's actions. To put this differently, if I drive on one side of the road but not on the other, that is no big issue. The same for other drivers. But if all drivers drive on the right-hand side of the road, then this creates an order to *traffic* (in the aggregate) that is beneficial to all: fewer accidents and faster travel. This order also affects individual drivers' decisions—it makes more sense to drive on the same side as everybody else, because doing otherwise would be unsafe and highly inefficient.

Similarly, what one entrepreneur does is important and might even be disruptive, as we saw with Henry Ford's Model T. But disruptive of what? Of the previously existing market order, which is the aggregate of producers' and consumers actions. Thus, entrepreneurs can *individually* act in certain ways (the corollary of individually driving on one side of the road) and in the *aggregate* create an order (right-lane driving) that benefits us all.

Let's elaborate for clarity. The entrepreneur imagines a new good or process that has not yet been tried. Henry Ford imagined an automobile using assembly line production, Johannes Gutenberg a printing press, and Thomas Edison a light bulb. The entrepreneur is convinced that the new good will bring more value to consumers than existing goods do. He believes that the potential value is so high that consumers will be willing to pay for his new good. In other words, he expects to make a profit.

The entrepreneur's profit calculation is based on the costs of available resources: salaries for workers, a production facility, materials and machines, electricity, etc. These costs are easy to estimate because the resources are available on the market—their prices have already been determined (this is important, and we'll come back to it). For resources that are hard to come by, an entrepreneur can estimate how much it will take to outbid other producers. The cost of building a new type of machine can also be estimated because everything that is needed is already available for purchase. Practically all the costs can be estimated in money prices, so an entrepreneur can easily estimate the cost of producing this new good.

Will it be worth it? Will the undertaking generate sufficient profit? To figure this out, the entrepreneur must estimate the *new good's value to consumers*. That value gives a rough idea of what prices consumers will be willing to pay and quantity sold at those prices. This price—derived from value—is the basis for an entrepreneur's decisions for how, when, and where to produce. Expected revenue *in money prices* constitutes the maximum an entrepreneur would be willing to pay workers, sellers of capital, etc. Subtracting the costs from the expected revenue gives the entrepreneur an idea of a product's profitability and its expected rate of return. This monetary calculation is possible because both cost and benefit are expressed in money—they can be compared and an outcome, even though it is in part based on guesses and estimates, albeit a predicted one, can be calculated. Based on the expected profit, the entrepreneur can then decide whether the investment is worthwhile. Monetary calculation allows for economizing on the market level!

This may sound obvious, but it is not. Many overlook the fact that it is the value outcome that guides entrepreneurs and informs their choices of how to run the business. Entrepreneurs are motivated by profits, which can be made when consumers value the good. Value is out of the entrepreneur's hands, in other words, but *cost is a choice.*

Consider the combined effect of all entrepreneurs making choices about costs based on their best guesses of the value they will provide consumers. They constantly bid for resources and reconsider their costs—in competition with each other. Just like the entrepreneur above, they might have to motivate workers or entice sellers of materials or services by offering a higher price. Even if they already have a business, they still need to choose whether to renew previous contracts, renegotiate them, revise production, etc. These choices and decisions are based on the expected value outcome: for entrepreneurs trying something new, this is their best guess of how much value consumers might see in their goods; for entrepreneurs continuing to produce an existing good, it might be their assumption that things will continue as before (or not!).

Those entrepreneurs who expect to produce more value can bid higher prices for inputs—and will find it easier to get the inputs they want. Those who expect to produce less value cannot afford to buy the most expensive inputs and will need to consider other, likely inferior, ones. This means the most useful and value-contributing resources will be sold at the highest prices and, therefore, be used where they are expected to create most value for consumers. Entrepreneurs thereby indirectly *direct resources* toward their "best" uses.

The bidding process is not only a way to direct resources to where they are expected to be most valuable, although this is very important. It also determines the market prices of those resources. There are already determined prices that entrepreneurs can use in their profitability calculations. To avoid losses, entrepreneurs will stay away from resources that are too expensive (which is a sign that the market expects someone else to create more value from them) and instead choose more affordable resources that can generate profit.

Thus, entrepreneurs' competitive bidding directs resources *and* determines their prices—and by extension *which projects should be pursued*. Only the projects with the highest expected value can be expected to earn a profit (and will therefore be pursued). An entrepreneur who anticipates creating new value can afford to outbid existing production.[2] This is why large corporations have little sway over entrepreneurs. What matters is the expected value contribution, not organizational size.

This curious process of market pricing of the means of production, in which entrepreneurs make decisions based on prices that they are also involved in determining, is what allows a market to use *scarce resources rationally*—that is economically from the perspective of future value outcome. This process does not create a perfect outcome, which is impossible because production decisions, including what costs to assume, always precede consumers' valuations. The outcome of any production is uncertain and ultimately depends on what consumers choose to buy. Remember, it is *a process*—it cannot be maximizing because the outcome is not and cannot be known, but it can be improved.

The uncertainty of the future explains why so many entrepreneurs fail. Without knowing the future, many of them will miscalculate, perhaps overestimate the consumer value of what they set out to produce.

---

[2]Entrepreneurs who do not have their own capital should be able to secure external funding if the expected value is high enough.

Nevertheless failed entrepreneurs make an important contribution because their failure both makes clear to other entrepreneurs what does not work and makes their resources available to other entrepreneurs.

This system works because it is based on private property: entrepreneurs personally gain or lose. If they did not risk losing their own money and property, many of them would be less careful in choosing which costs to bear, and prices would as a result not be rational value estimations. If entrepreneurs did not stand to gain from their uncertain undertakings, they would have little reason to try them—and even less reason to choose their costs wisely.

In sum, the market process rationally distributes scarce resources because entrepreneurs risk their own personal property and therefore do their best to make the right choices. If they fail, they are mercilessly weeded out and have less capital to try again. Those entrepreneurs who are successful, who chose their costs wisely and produced goods that consumers valued highly, are rewarded with profits. This entrepreneurial dynamic creates a "division of intellectual labor" where the best and brightest can try their ideas—and benefit consumers.

## Entrepreneurship and Management

The market process, as outlined here, is so much more than what we can observe at any moment. Because it is a process, everything that exists at any given time is the result of what came before—and will be challenged by what will come after. In other words, the firms that exist today are the outcome of the market's weeding-out process—they "won" the entrepreneurial bidding for resources. Had consumers chosen differently or entrepreneurs had other ideas, there would be other businesses producing other goods.

Similarly, some of the entrepreneurs that are currently in the process of securing funding, starting up their businesses, or experimenting with production processes are creating tomorrow's businesses. Existing producers will only stay in business if they continue to create value—and create *more* value than tomorrow's businesses. This is why existing businesses, even the very big ones, cannot sit back and relax but must innovate. They have a place in the market process only as long as no one else offers consumers more value.

In other words, if we were to analyze the economy and focus only on the businesses that exist, we would miss most of the process! We would not be able to understand why these businesses (and the goods they produce) exist, and we would not understand how or why entrepreneurs with better ideas might soon replace them. Looking only at the status quo—the economy that we can observe in the present—or the changes that have happened in the recent past, we could easily conclude that the economy is a fairly static system that is far from maximizing the use of resources. It would be easy to find inefficiencies and come up with other potential solutions. But this would be an enormous mistake. The market process is primarily about figuring out how to create new value for consumers—it is not about maximizing output in current production.

It is an *entrepreneurial* process. The status quo is merely the most recent expression of the process—it's yesterday's winners before they are replaced by tomorrow's. The market process is in constant flux and is characterized by renewal and progress.

The market process goes well beyond simple *production management*. We should want businesses to have good management that streamline production, cut costs, and tweak and improve the goods they produce. But management is what takes place in production after the entrepreneur has been proven right. As Mises put it, the manager is the "junior partner" of the entrepreneur.

Simply put, management solves an entirely different problem than entrepreneurship. It is about maximizing the outcome of a production process (typically in terms of profit). It is a fundamental error to misconstrue the market process as mere production management.

PART III

# Intervention

CHAPTER 8

# Monetary Intervention

## THE BOOM-BUST CYCLE

The economy's constant flux is not random change but adjustments to the production apparatus in the pursuit of creating value. Value is a moving target because consumers want change over time and innovations and new opportunities. The constant adjustments mean the market is best understood as a process.

There are two fundamental tendencies in this. First, there are the adjustments made to existing production intended to keep efforts aligned with expected consumer value. Without these, production would become ever more misaligned with what consumers want. We would see falling living standards as a result.

Second, entrepreneurs try innovations that they imagine will create new value for consumers. When these are successful, they disrupt and replace already existing production. When production is revolutionized in this way, the economy grows and our standards of living rise.

The overall process is dependent on a functioning price system, which provides economic actors with the information they need to respond rationally to changes (we saw how this works in chapter 7). However, if prices are manipulated and give false information, entrepreneurs will make decisions on that faulty information. This means entrepreneurs are more likely to fail in their undertakings, but it also means entrepreneurs' actions introduce errors into the production apparatus. The economy, as a result, becomes *distorted*.

The boom-bust cycle is a particular type of distortion in which manipulated price signals bring about malinvestments that produce an artificial, unsustainable boom followed by a bust as the errors in production become apparent.

## THE RATE OF RETURN AND CAPITAL INVESTMENTS

For any investment, it is important to think of the expected return as a rate rather than an amount. Why? Because it is the relative outcome that determines how good the investment is. A $1 million profit is not much if it comes from a billion-dollar investment. But $1 million is an enormous return if the original investment was $100,000. The profit in dollars is the same, but the latter is ten thousand times as much as the former.[1]

---

[1] A profit of $1 million from an investment of $1 billion is a 0.1 percent return, but on a $100,000 investment, it is a 1,000 percent return. Thus, if the $1 billion were instead invested in smaller projects at a 1,000 percent return, it would generate $10 billion in total profits. That's ten thousand times the profit of the large investment.

Thinking of profit in terms of rates of return makes it easier to compare different projects. It means an entrepreneur—and investors in the entrepreneur's business—can compare alternatives that are different in every way. For example, a new airline would require a massive capital investment to acquire the planes, hire crews, and get access to airports, whereas a new lawn service requires a much smaller initial investment. But it could be that the larger investment is still expected to provide a much higher *rate* of return, which means that it makes more economic sense—even though it requires much more capital.

As we've discussed, market profits correlate with consumer value. An investment earns a higher return *because* of its greater value to consumers. This means we are all better off if the investments made get as high returns as possible.

A higher rate of return also means an entrepreneur can more easily borrow investment capital. Consequently, very capital-intensive projects (such as an airline) can still get the needed financing even though they are very expensive up front. And the entrepreneur can easily calculate whether the cost of capital is worth it. For example, if a project's return will be 7 percent and a loan from the bank can be had at 5 percent interest, then the expected net gain is 2 percent. It means the entrepreneur can also compare this net 2 percent with, for example, what a much less capital-intensive investment (such as a lawn service) would earn—even if he would then not need external financing. If the lawn service is expected to provide a net return of 4 percent, the entrepreneur would not choose to start an airline.

Its rate of return is only half of what he can make from his lawn service (2 instead of 4 percent).

But imagine if the interest rate were only 1 percent. Now the airline's return is *50 percent higher*[2] than the lawn service's, even though nothing else has changed. In this situation, we would expect entrepreneurs to start airlines rather than lawn services because that is where they will make more money—despite taking out loans for the investment. It takes more productive capital to start an airline, but this is not an issue at the lower interest rate.

If the difference between the rates of return is high enough, we might also see entrepreneurs sell or discontinue their lawn services to instead run airlines and other more capital-intensive businesses. This would be an appropriate economizing shift in investment because the airline industry provides more expected value to consumers (reflected in its higher rate of return). The existing capital would be invested where it can be used most productively in the service of consumers.

A higher rate of return is not only due to lower costs. It can also be the result of higher value creation. Lower costs and higher value creation can both increase the rate and vice versa. It is the expected bottom line relative to the investment needed that counts when making investment decisions.

However, even if the projects' expected net rates of return are the same, their economic situations may not

---

[2] The return on the lawn service remains 4 percent, whereas the airline's expected rate of return is now 7 percent less the cost of the capital at 1 percent. That's 50 percent more than the lawn service (6%/4%=150%).

be. This is another example of how the market empowers actors by lowering the bar: an entrepreneur does not need to know *why* the rate of return is high to make an investment. But it makes a difference when we try to understand the economy. For example, when the interest rate is 5 percent, an 11 percent expected return on highly capital-intensive investments in air travel makes their net return 50 percent higher than the 4 percent return on lawn services.

But the economy is different. In the case of an 11 percent return and a 5 percent interest rate, the high rate of return is due to high expected value creation. The high interest rate suggests capital is scarce, which is why banks can charge a high interest rate. To attract investments—and therefore capital—airlines are expected to create more value. We saw this above: when airlines' rate of return was only 7 percent, lawn services earned a higher net rate of return. When airlines' rate of return rose to 11 percent, lawn services earned a lower net rate of return than airlines. Investors were then incentivized to pull their money from lawn services and other investments and put it in airlines to earn higher profits. This activity shifts capital that is already in use toward better (more value-creative) uses: consumers gain as more value is produced using *the same* resources.

In the case of a 7 percent return and a 1 percent interest rate, the interest rate is lower because there is *more* capital available for investments. There is more capital available because people have chosen to consume less and instead save more for the future. So production of consumption goods also falls. The economy therefore can support *more* investments in addition to those that are already underway. Consumers gain as more capital is invested toward producing goods (which will be available in the future). The lower interest rate allows unused capital to be put to use, although this does not preclude shifts from other lines of production. The added investments increase the overall output of the economy.

The rate of return is simply an indication of an investment's added value. It does not matter whether this rate changes due to fluctuations in cost (lower interest rates) or in value (higher expected ticket sales). What matters to the entrepreneur is the expected rate of return, which approximates the relative value added to the economy. Higher value production and lower production costs both benefit consumers.

## The Cause and Nature of the Artificial Boom

Imagine that the interest rate falls, as above, from 5 to 1 percent but there is not more capital available to invest. How could that happen? If banks create new currency and offer it as loans, then the interest rates they charge will be competitively bid down, pushing the market interest rate below where it otherwise would be (for example, 1 percent instead of 5 percent). But this is not a matter of different economic conditions—there is not more capital available, only more money in the form of loans, to buy the resources that entrepreneurs need to start and finish their production projects. So, the interest rate signal that entrepreneurs rely on for economic calculation is *artificially* low. Therefore their decisions and actions will be based on this faulty signal.

As above, the lower interest rate means more investments. In our example, entrepreneurs will create new airlines (and expand existing airlines' operations), as this industry appears more profitable, relatively speaking. As entrepreneurs with borrowed purchasing power (the new money) flow into the market and attempt to establish new production, they increase demand for capital and bid up prices. As these investments happen primarily in the capital-intensive airline industry, demand increases specifically for planes, crews, and other resources used in this industry. Thus, airplanes' price tags are higher and airline employees, pilots, and flight crews will earn higher salaries.

Their customers' increasing willingness to pay signals airplane manufacturers to ramp up their production. As the manufacturers place orders for aluminum and other materials, and start hiring more engineers, their bids for those resources increase their respective prices as well. This causes a boom in investments, and prices go up across the stages of production: airlines, then plane manufacturers, then aluminum producers, then miners. Each stage sees increased demand, which means producers can charge higher prices and earn higher profits, which motivates them to further expand their operations. These conditions also motivate other entrepreneurs to invest in these industries to capture part of the profits. These increased investments are all appropriate, given the signals: the prices go up, suggesting the supply was inadequate; producers underestimated the demand.

The new and expanding airlines, which are more willing and able to pay, outcompete other users of those resources. Other commercial aluminum users, such as soft drink producers, face higher prices and lower availability, which affects their profit margins. In response to the higher prices, these producers re-evaluate their plans to economize on their aluminum use and consider alternatives. As a result, soft drink prices could go up or soft drinks might start to appear in glass or plastic containers instead of aluminum cans.

That the aluminum that would have been available to soft drink producers is being redirected toward airplane manufacturing is not as crazy as it might seem. This is where the aluminum, according to the market's price signals, should create most value for consumers.[3] We would expect proper market prices to shift production toward where it does most good as entrepreneurs compete to satisfy consumers (as we saw in chapter 7).

But there is a problem: the higher prices in airplane production result from the artificially low interest rate brought about by banks' creating new money and expanding credit—not greater availability of capital. Therefore, the whole shift in the economy toward airplace production, including all investments made to support this production, and therefore *away from* other lines of production that appear relatively less profitable, constitutes malinvestment.

Malinvestment means that investments are structurally distorted: some areas of the economy see overinvestment whereas others see underinvestment. The

---

[3]Our example assumes soft drink producers do not expect sufficient (higher) demand to expand production, but if they did, they too might exploit the lower interest rate to invest in expanding output through, for example, automation. This would further increase demand in the higher stages of production, as both airplane manufacturers and soft drink producers bid to acquire more aluminum.

overinvestment in airlines also means overinvestment in airplane manufacturing, aluminum production, and mining, intended to meet expectations of higher demand. These investments are made to increase production capacity to meet the expected greater demand for air travel (due to its greater anticipated value). As investments soar and prices go up in anticipation of the higher demand, these industries experience a boom.

These same industries, at least in our example, also expanded in the same manner when the interest fell due to greater availability of productive capital. The difference is that this new expansion is using resources that are not readily available but rather are being shifted away from other industries where consumer demand remains largely unchanged. The change is therefore not a matter of the economy shifting from one line of production to another in response to expected changes in what consumers value. Instead, there is a greater demand for productive capital and labor *overall* as entrepreneurs establish new lines of production, motivated by the artificially lower interest rate.

From the perspective of consumer value, this boom is caused by overinvestment, in response to the faulty signal, in airlines and those higher-stage production processes that support expanding air travel, *and*, therefore, relative underinvestment in other lines of production. Artificial booms like this, caused by the expansion of credit, can occur in longer production projects in general. Such overall malinvestments distort the economy's production apparatus: the outputs are no longer aligned with what consumers want most (as imagined by entrepreneurs).

## THE TURNING POINT

The boom is unsustainable because it largely consists of *mal*investments, not because the economy grows rapidly. What we call the business cycle is the sequence of an unsustainable boom followed by the inevitable bust—a bubble that then bursts. This is different from the sound progression of an economy. It helps to contrast the two.

First, let us look at sustainable growth. We saw above that the interest rate reflects the availability of capital for productive investment. When more capital is made available, the interest rate falls, and vice versa. Specifically, this happens when consumers are less eager to buy and consume goods in the present and prefer to save a greater portion of their wealth for the future. Their *time preference* is lower, meaning they have longer time horizons in their valuations— they look more to the future than before. As a result, entrepreneurs that produce consumer goods face falling demand and lower profitability, and therefore have an incentive to scale down their operations and look for other opportunities. Some of them may go out of business. As a result, entrepreneurs overall reduce the production and sale of consumption goods.

This frees up productive capital for new investments, which are now feasible and increasingly profitable, as the increased savings force the interest rate down. So entrepreneurs invest more in production processes that produce goods that will be available for sale in the future. Overall, this shifts productive capacity away from production for present consumption to production for future consumption. Entrepreneurs are responding to price signals and abandoning production with low profitability to seek the higher expected rates of return in production for the future. This is quite in line with consumers consuming less and saving more (they are postponing consumption). In fact, the shift in production is a matter of adjusting production to where it is expected to produce greater benefit for consumers.

The unsustainable boom is different. Here, entrepreneurs increase investments in production for future consumption based on the artificially lowered interest rate. In other words, there has been no corresponding shift in consumer behavior—instead, the lower interest rate makes consumers less eager to save (they earn lower interest on their postponed consumption) and thus encourages consumption in the present. This causes tension in the production structure, between production that serves present consumption (which is going up) and investments that serve future consumption (which is expected to go up).

On the one hand, entrepreneurs producing for present consumption see no falling demand because consumers have not shifted away from consuming. Their products' profitability is not falling so why would they cut back their activities? Thus, these entrepreneurs continue to compete for inputs and keep placing orders for them.

At the same time, the lower interest rate causes an increase in investments for future production. The higher stages of production experience greatly increased demand as they receive orders from both the production processes serving consumers in the present *and* those undertaken to serve them in the future. Remember, all of this is based on the faulty signal. As there is not more capital available but there are many more buyers, the prices are bid up to very high levels. This is sometimes called an asset price bubble.

Although competition between the new future-oriented and the old present-oriented may seem like a good thing, the faulty signal pulls the economy in different directions. The prices of production factors are bid up as a result of the overinvestment in the higher stages of production (in our example, airplanes, aluminum, mining). These price increases are based on the faulty signal and therefore detached from genuine expected future demand for air travel. These price increases include wages for workers in these stages, who then have more money to spend on present consumption. With an artificially lowered interest rate, there is less incentive to postpone consumption. Therefore, a greater fraction of earned wages, which are now also higher because of the boom, is spent on consumption goods—increasing demand for goods in the present too.

In sum, sustainable growth is caused and supported by a shift in consumer behavior: decreased demand for consumption in the present that makes capital available for investment in the higher stages of production. In the unsustainable boom, in contrast, there is no shift but rather *added* investments without additional productive capital. Thus, the production structure reflects higher demand for consumer goods both in the present *and* the future, based on the assumption that there are sufficient capital goods available to complete all these new production projects. Another way of putting this is that the economy, through the actions of entrepreneurs who were deceived and misled by the artificially low interest rate, both consumes and invests the capital that is available. It should be obvious that this is not possible. There is not enough productive capital to support both.

The unsustainable boom is thus based on production that requires resources that do not exist. Many of those production processes, especially in the higher orders (far from consumers), cannot be completed because the capital necessary is too scarce. This does not mean that factories suddenly find themselves without resources, although shortages may occur. More likely, asset prices are bid to such high levels that many investments no longer appear profitable. Entrepreneurs then discover that they have made significant errors in their calculations and are forced to abandon their investments.

Entrepreneurial error is commonplace in the market, but the errors do not usually cause boom-bust cycles. What is unique to the business cycle is that there is a massive *cluster* of simultaneous entrepreneurial errors. The reason, as we saw above, is that entrepreneurs have been misled into acting as though there were capital available for their production projects. But there is not. The expansion of credit, not availability of capital, lowered the interest rate to a level that does not reflect the real availability of capital for investment.

This raises the question of why entrepreneurs allow themselves to be fooled. Do they not realize that the interest rate is artificially low? Maybe they do. But this does not matter because they still expect to benefit from the lower cost of borrowing. Why would they not pursue projects that they expect to be profitable? Even if they were familiar with business cycle theory and knew that the economy is in a bubble, the bubble is in fact highly profitable. To not expand one's business as the bubble inflates is akin to turning down profits. This may not sound like a huge problem, but a business's investors will likely feel differently. Also, competitors cannot be expected to turn down profits, so inaction could allow them to expand their market share. As a result, not expanding during the bubble is to risk one's business.

There is also the issue of the inflow of entrepreneurs during a bubble. As prices rise, more people see an opportunity to earn profits—and a reason to leave their current employment. Thus, the boom lures those who would otherwise not enter the market as investors. Their lack of experience suggests they are more prone to make errors and thereby contribute to overall malinvestments.

## The Corrective Bust

The bust comes quickly. Even though the bubble itself might be easy to spot, it is difficult to predict exactly when it will burst. The actual turning point can be triggered by seemingly unrelated events that put additional strain on specific malinvestments and cause them to fail. As the production apparatus is already strained by high demand yet firmly high prices, one failing business can easily drag down its customers and suppliers, who can no longer expect to be paid for services rendered.

This causes a cascade of failures that reveals the extent of the malinvestments in the economy.

The mass of failing investments, and therefore failing businesses and jobs lost, is the bust. But note that the bust is not a separate phenomenon: it is already embedded in the boom, whose investments are unsustainable. This is why we refer to the boom-bust sequence as a cycle: the malinvestments that cause the boom must be undone for the economy to get back on track. It is *not* the case that the boom is a sound development and that the bust is avoidable; the boom is not real economic growth but an illusion. Consumers expected something else. Entrepreneurs made investments that were not motivated by genuine value expectations but facilitated by a corrupted signal of capital availability: the artificially low interest rate.

The bust releases the capital goods malinvested in processes that do not serve consumers so that they can be invested where they can do more good. In other words, other entrepreneurs get a chance to acquire the capital to pursue consumer value—the failures are necessary for the malinvestments to be revealed and then replaced by sound productive investments.

For the bust to restore sound production, however, the interest rate must be allowed to increase. If it is kept artificially low, this will only prolong the corrective process, as the new entrepreneurs will also be misled and structural errors therefore persist.

CHAPTER 9

# Regulatory Intervention

By regulations, we mean restrictions imposed on the economy by government: prohibitions, license requirements, quality or safety standards, price controls, quotas, and subsidies, etc. Although they differ in their specifics and in their stated purposes, they are all implemented to induce a change in the economy.

If regulations do not change anything, they are ineffective. This is because the specific restrictions are inapplicable or they are not enforced in practice. The point, however, is that all regulations are *intended* to impose some change and that they matter only if and to the extent that they do. Effective regulations, successful in producing the intended outcome or not, change behaviors and therefore the structure of the economy.

Some regulations are imposed on producers, whereas others target consumer behavior. The former may impose additional costs or prohibitions on some producers or artificially lower the costs of others. The purpose is to change the types of production projects undertaken and therefore the goods made available to consumers. The latter seek to change consumers' behavior, which in turn affects producers because they must respond to the changed nature and structure of demand. In both cases, therefore, the outcome is a change in the economy's production structure.

We know that the production structure is determined by entrepreneurs seeking to profit from satisfying consumer wants (chapter 5). Thus, for regulations to be effective, they must affect entrepreneurs' behavior and change which production projects they choose to undertake. The observable outcome (what is *seen*), what did not occur as a result (the counterfactual or *unseen*), and the longer-term effects (the *unrealized*) are key to understanding the impact of regulations.

## The Seen

The observable world is the obvious starting point to analyze a regulation's effects but it can also be misleading. It is obvious because it is what we can see and measure. But studing it also leads to errors and premature conclusions because although the actual economy—its *data*—appears to provide straightforward facts about a regulation's effects, it actually does not.

In a world in which a newly imposed regulation is the *only* change that takes place, we could easily compare the state of the economy before and after and thereby assess its effect. However, as the market is a process that is in constant flux, the regulation is decidedly *not* the only change—it is an imposition on the market's ongoing unfolding and evolution.

Consider the case of imposing a minimum wage, which stipulates a price floor in the market. For such a regulation to be effective, its stipulated wage must be higher than what employers already pay. If the market wage is $10 per hour, the minimum wage must require that employers pay some higher amount—it must impose a penalty on or prohibit employers from paying a wage lower than the wage stipulated.

If the imposed minimum wage requires that employers pay $14 per hour, then that is the wage in the open market. Anything else would be illegal. Thus before and after comparisons would make it seem like people make more money after the imposition of the minimum wage. But do they? To figure this out, we must also consider what would have been the situation had a minimum wage requirement not been imposed— the counterfactual, or the unseen.

## THE UNSEEN

The "unseen" refers to the "other side" of the story— what otherwise would have happened. Since it does not happen, we cannot measure it. Yet it is the cost of any action or choice. If I choose steak for dinner, I forego all other possibilities I could have had instead. The highest value of those possibilities is the economic cost of the choice—the tradeoff is the value foregone.

Without a counterfactual, we look only at the presumed benefit but do not consider the cost. Thus, the analysis becomes one-sided, and we risk missing something important. We also cannot determine if it was a good or bad choice. Was it *worth it*? We need to know the cost to answer this question.

This applies also to regulations like the minimum wage in the example above. The typical purpose for a minimum wage is to raise workers' wages. Considering only the seen would make the regulation seem successful, because after the minimum wage has been imposed there would be no one who makes less than $14 per hour. This would be a premature conclusion because we have not yet looked at the unseen.

We must thus ask what would have happened had that minimum wage not been imposed. It is important to recognize that the minimum wage does not magically raise wages but compels employers to not employ anyone for less than the stipulated wage. This is not the same thing as raising workers' wages.

Let us consider an example of an employer who before the minimum wage is imposed has three employees. They are paid $7, $10, and $16 per hour respectively. The reason for their different wages is that their value contributions to the employer are not the same. The worker being paid $7 per hour is in job training, learning the trade, which explains the low wage. Once trained, and more valuable to the employer, the employee would expect to earn a higher wage in the future. The worker being paid $16 has a unique skillset that is particularly important to the employer's line of production, making their contribution greater. This worker could easily get a job elsewhere if he was paid less. The worker earning $10 has no special expertise beyond job experience and therefore makes the market wage for regular workers, commensurate with his value contribution in the production process.

The employer would be unwilling to pay any of these workers more than their value contribution. They are employed for contributing to the value created, not subtracting from it. Paying them anything else would be charity—consumption, not production. The workers do not make less than their value contribution, either, because if they did, other employers could profitablity hire them at a higher wage.

Now suppose a $14 per hour minimum wage is imposed. This means the employer is no longer allowed to pay anyone less than $14 per hour. The employer must decide whether to double the wage of the worker in training and raise the $10 per hour worker's wage by almost half. The third worker, who already makes $16 per hour, is not directly affected. The employer is likely to let the worker in training go, because his productivity is lower than a regular worker's—but his price is now the same.

The employer cannot afford to simply raise the $10 worker's wage because his value contribution is more than $10 but less than $14. But by tweaking the production process, cutting benefits, and abolishing other perks, such as afternoon coffee breaks, this worker can be kept at the higher rate of $14. At least for now.

The seen, therefore, is that this employer paid an average wage of $11 per hour before the regulation was put in place and $15 per hour after. An obvious gain! The regulation worked. It magically raised workers' wages.

The unseen, however, paints a different picture. If nothing had happened in the economy to change worker productivity or the profitability of the business, there would be three workers employed at a total of $33 per hour. Now there are two workers at a total of $30 per hour instead. Also, the lower-paid employee is now working harder to justify his higher wage.

Was the imposed regulation worth it? Economics cannot answer this question because it is a value judgment. But it can identify the regulation's result and, therefore, show whether the regulation fulfilled its promise of raising workers' wages (it did, for one worker; but it also resulted in another worker being laid off).

There is more to the story, because the seen and the unseen only consider effects in the present. However, as we now know, the economy is a process—the world we live in today has implications for the future too.

## THE UNREALIZED

Understanding that the market is a process provides further insight into the real effect of regulations on the economy beyond the seen and the unseen. To see how, we will continue the minimum wage example and work through the logic step by step with and without the regulation.

After the minimum wage has been imposed, the worker in training is laid off. Rather than making some money and gaining the experience necessary to propel his career, he is now looking for a job. However, as all employers are compelled to pay $14 per hour, the threshold to get a job is much steeper than before. Without training the worker just starting out cannot find a job where he would contribute at least that much to the bottom line, and since he also cannot get the experience that would increase his productivity, he remains unemployed.

Meanwhile the workers who retained their jobs are increasingly frustrated. The highest-paid workers feel unfairly treated because they did not receive a raise while the less productive colleagues received a 40 percent increase for no obvious reason. And now pressure to perform is higher too, and the more skilled worker is expected to assist the less skilled worker to make production run smoothly. It was better when there were three workers even though the third worker was still learning the trade. Now the two of them are struggling to produce what the three of them produced easily before.

The skilled worker, in turn, believes he earned a raise and is bitter about losing some benefits he used to enjoy. He remembers when he could take a coffee break, talk to colleagues, relax, and de-stress. It is more difficult to keep up now and he feels worn out as the weekend nears. Not to mention that the worker has been told not to expect a raise for the foreseeable future because his productivity does not warrant a higher pay.

This is the seen with an imposed minimum wage of $14 per hour.

In the counterfactual world, where there is no minimum wage, all three workers remain employed. Initially they are paid the same as before: $7, $10, and $16 per hour, respectively. But as the worker in training gains experience, his productivity increases, and the employer raises his wage, first to $8 and then to $10 when he's as productive as other workers on the job market. Why would the employer raise the wage? Stepped raises may have been contracted earlier. Or maybe the employer wants to pay the worker a fair wage because otherwise he would look for and get gainful employment elsewhere.

The other two workers also increase their productivity and get raises. The employer can afford this because he did not have to increase one person's wage by 40 percent but also because the workers produce greater value. The workers are paid higher wages because they contribute greater value and therefore contribute to the combined wealth and well-being of company, and society in general. So soon, they are paid $10, $12, and $17 per hour, respectively—a total of $39 per hour, an 18 percent increase paid for by increased production.

But this is still not the whole story. The wages earned by the three workers are their purchasing power, which they use to buy goods others produce. The workers' demand, a result of their contribution to supply, makes revenue in other businesses possible.

We can now see that the difference between the seen and the unseen—the regulation's cost—is not merely the unemployed worker. This is the immediate effect, which reduces total output but increases the marginal wage and output (by excluding the worker with the lowest productivity). However, what is also lost is the experience that this worker would have gained, and therefore his increased productivity over time. His future jobs and perhaps his career are lost. His increased production is also lost, and therefore the value he would have created for consumers, who will not be able to purchase those goods.

The unrealized are all those valuable opportunities that never come to be because of the regulation: the value of the goods that would have been produced, the trainee's career, the workers' demand for goods. The economy is on an overall lower-value trajectory, which means the loss is all the value that would have otherwise been attained.

This shouldn't be surprising, because free-market production, albeit imperfect, is driven by entrepreneurs seeking to profit from serving consumers. When this order is upset, entrepreneurs cannot pursue what they expect will be the highest-value uses of scarce resources. This means that the most productive projects—including the job opportunities they create, at wages based on the expected value contribution, *and* the highest-value goods for consumers—will be lost. The unrealized is the true cost of regulations, and it far exceeds the unseen.

# Conclusion:
# Action and Interaction

Nothing about the market economy is magic. As I have attempted to show, the market is quite real and mundane. It functions in a certain and knowable way; it has a specific behavior, which emerges from and arises out of people's actions and interactions.

We refer to this behavior as *economic laws*, which are laws in the same sense as the laws of physics. There is no way to escape them. They are immutable.

Critics claim markets have no nature, there are no economic laws or they do not always apply. They sometimes claim markets are or must be designed and work in an "institutional vacuum." But this is a misunderstanding. Changing circumstances will change the *outcome* of the market process, but markets do not function differently regardless of the institutional setting.

The specific goods and services produced, the number of job opportunities, the distribution of value created, and so on are not caused *only* by economic laws. But they certainly are subject to those laws. All else equal, a higher price for a good means less of it will be sold than otherwise would be the case. This does not mean other influences have no effect.

For example, if the government required everyone to buy some good this coming month, the quantity demanded would increase even as that good's price rose. The same would be the case if instead of an imposed requirement, a new fad made a lot of people eager to purchase that good. In neither case are economic laws being evaded or out of play. On the contrary, both outcomes are well in line with economic laws but contingent on the specific change.

Therefore, we *must* understand economic laws to understand the market economy and the evolution of the market process. It is only through proper economic reasoning that we can uncover the economy's actual workings and make sense of the market process. If you now understand that, then I have been successful.

Specific outcomes are impossible to understand—not to mention predict—unless we first understand how markets work. This means *economic literacy* is a necessary starting point for effective policy making. Regulations, which we discussed in chapter 9, must take economic laws into account.

If we do not understand the market economy, we cannot understand the effects regulations will have—and chances are they will not only be ineffective but destructive.

Economic literacy is the antidote to destructive policy. But it is so much more. Economic literacy is mind-opening because it allows us to truly understand how the world works.

# Further Reading

## BOOKS FOR BEGINNERS

Ammous, Saifedean. *Principles of Economics*. Amman, Jordan: The Saif House, 2023.

Bastiat, Frédéric. *That Which Is Seen and That Which Is Not Seen* (1850). In vol. 1 of *The Bastiat Collection*, 1–48. Auburn, AL: Ludwig von Mises Institute, 2007.

Bylund, Per L. *The Seen, the Unseen, and the Unrealized: How Regulations Affect Our Everyday Lives*. Lanham, MD: Lexington Books, 2016.

Hazlitt, Henry. *Economics in One Lesson*. New York: Three Rivers Press, 1979.

Murphy, Robert P. *Choice: Cooperation, Enterprise, and Human Action*. Oakland, CA: Independent Institute, 2015.

## ECONOMICS TREATISES

Menger, Carl. *Principles of Economics*. Translated by James Dingwall and Bert F. Hoselitz. Auburn, AL: Ludwig von Mises Institute, 2007.

Mises, Ludwig von. *Human Action: A Treatise on Economics*, scholar's ed. Auburn, AL: Ludwig von Mises Institute, 1998.

Rothbard, *Man, Economy and State: A Treatise on Economic Principles*. 2 vols. Princeton, NJ: D. Van Nostrand, 1962.

## ENTREPRENEURSHIP AND ECONOMIC GROWTH

Bylund, Per L. *The Problem of Production: A New Theory of the Firm*. London: Routledge, 2016.

Foss, Nicolai J., and Peter G. Klein. *Organizing Entrepreneurial Judgment: A New Approach to the Firm*. Cambridge: Cambridge University Press, 2015.

Kirzner, Israel M. *Competition and Entrepreneurship*. Chicago: University of Chicago Press, 1973.

Schumpeter, Joseph A. *Theory of Economic Development: An Inquiry into Profits, Capital, Credit, Interest, and the Business Cycle*. Translated by Redvers Opie. Cambridge, MA: Harvard University Press, 1934.

## ECONOMIC CALCULATION AND SOCIALISM

Boettke, Peter J. *Calculation and Coordination: Essays on Socialism and Transitional Political Economy*. London: Routledge, 2001.

Hoff, Trygve J. B. *Economic Calculation in the Socialist Society*. Indianapolis, IN: Liberty Press, 1981.

Huerta de Soto, Jesús. *Socialism, Economic Calculation, and Entrepreneurship*. Translated by Melinda Stroup. Cheltenham, UK: Edward Elgar, 2010.

Mises, Ludwig von. *Socialism: An Economic and Sociological Analysis.* Translated by J. Kahane. new ed. New Haven, CT: Yale University Press, 1951.

## MONEY AND BANKING

Lavoie, Donald. *Rivalry and Central Planning: The Socialist Calculation Debate Reconsidered.* Cambridge: Cambridge University Press, 1985.

Menger, Carl. *On the Origins of Money.* Translated by C. A. Foley. Auburn, AL: Ludwig von Mises Institute, 2009.

Mises, Ludwig von. *Bureaucracy.* New Haven, CT: Yale University Press, 1944.

Mises, Ludwig von. *The Theory of Money and Credit.* Translated by J. E. Batson. Auburn, AL: Ludwig von Mises Institute, 2009.

Rothbard, Murray N. *The Mystery of Banking.* 2nd ed. Auburn, AL: Ludwig von Mises Institute, 2008.

Rothbard, Murray N. *What Has Government Done to Our Money?* 5th ed. Auburn, AL: Ludwig von Mises Institute, 2010.

Salerno, Joseph T. *Money: Sound and Unsound.* Auburn, AL: Ludwig von Mises Institute, 2010.

## CAPITAL THEORY AND PRODUCTION

Böhm-Bawerk, Eugen von. *Capital and Interest: A Critical History of Economical Theory.* Translated by William Smart. London: Macmillan, 1890.

Garrison, Roger W. *Time and Money: The Macroeconomics of Capital Structure.* London: Routledge, 2000.

Hayek, Friedrich A. *Prices and Production.* 2nd ed. New York: Augustus M. Kelly, 1935.

Hayek, Friedrich A. *The Pure Theory of Capital.* Auburn, AL: Ludwig von Mises Institute, 2009.

Kirzner, Israel M. *An Essay on Capital.* New York: Augustus M. Kelley, 1996.

Lachmann, Ludwig M. *Capital and Its Structure.* Kansas City, KS: Sheed Andrews and McMeel, 1978.

Lewin, Peter. *Capital in Disequilibrium: The Role of Capital in a Changing World.* Abingdon, Oxfordshire, UK: Routledge, 1998.

## BUSINESS CYCLES

Ebeling, Richard M., ed. *The Austrian Theory of the Trade Cycle and Other Essays.* Auburn, AL: Ludwig von Mises Institute, 1996.

Huerta de Soto, Jesús. *Money, Bank Credit, and Economic Cycles*, translated by Melinda A. Stroup, 4th ed. Auburn, AL: Ludwig von Mises Institute, 2020.

Mises, Ludwig von. *The Theory of Money and Credit.* Translated by J. E. Batson. Auburn, AL: Ludwig von Mises Institute, 2009.

Rothbard, Murray N. *America's Great Depression.* 5th ed. Auburn, AL: Mises Institute, 2000.

Rothbard, Murray N. *The Panic of 1819: Reactions and Policies.* Auburn, AL: Ludwig von Mises Institute, 2007.

Temin, Peter. *Lessons from the Great Depression.* Cambridge, MA: MIT Press, 1991.

## METHOD AND ECONOMIC REASONING

Gordon, David. *An Introduction to Economic Reasoning*. Auburn, AL: Ludwig von Mises Institute, 2000.

Hoppe, Hans-Hermann. *Economic Science and the Austrian Method*. Auburn, AL: Ludwig von Mises Institute, 2007.

Mises, Ludwig von. *Theory and History: An Interpretation of Social and Economic Evolution*. Auburn, AL: Ludwig von Mises Institute, 2007.

Mises, Ludwig von. *The Ultimate Foundations of Economic Science: An Essay on Method*. New York: D. Van Nostrand, 1962.

Selgin, George A. *Praxeology and Understanding: An Analysis of the Controversy in Austrian Economics*. Auburn, AL: Ludwig von Mises Institute, 1990.

# Index